10654322

Pelican Books
Studies in Social Pathology
Editor: G. M. Carstairs

STUDENT CASUALTIES

Anthony Ryle

Student Casualties

Penguin Books

Penguin Books Ltd, Harmondsworth,
Middlesex, England
Penguin Books Inc., 7110 Ambassador Road,
Baltimore, Maryland 21207, U.S.A.
Penguin Books Australia Ltd, Ringwood,
Victoria, Australia

First published by Allen Lane The Penguin Press 1969
Published in Pelican Books 1973
Copyright © Anthony Ryle, 1969

Made and printed in Great Britain by
Cox & Wyman Ltd,
London, Reading and Fakenham
Set in Intertype Times

Contents

Editorial Foreword

Until comparatively recent times, higher education was a privilege restricted to a very limited élite. It is easy to forget that less than a century ago more than half the population of England was illiterate. Elementary education became universally available by an Act of Parliament of 1870, but two generations later, during the First World War, a substantial minority of the population still could not read or write. During the Second World War, Rab Butler's Education Act brought secondary education within the reach of many who previously could not afford it; but it was only in the post-war years, and particularly in the 1960s that university education began to be attainable – at least in theory – by all young people who had the necessary intelligence.

These changes, which have been accelerated by the demands of an increasingly sophisticated technology, have had inevitable repercussions on university life. Not only are universities more numerous, and in some cases larger than ever before; their student bodies, too, are very different. Although university students still represent less than ten per cent of their age group, they are no longer a small, pampered group. They have earned their privilege by virtue of their brains and hard work; and they are not allowed to forget that each one who graduates does so after incurring an expense of several thousands of pounds in public money.

Being members of a meritocracy carries certain penalties. Students, especially those in the most sought-after universities, are aware of the strain of having to justify their privileged

state. Their university years are a testing time, because success
in their degree courses may have an important influence on
their subsequent careers. They can only make the best use of
these critical years if they enjoy good physical and mental
health. Fortunately, nowadays most young people do keep well.
As recently as the 1940s, tuberculosis was still a serious hazard;
but this has almost disappeared. Today, accidents are the commonest threats to life among students; but among the ailments
which can interfere with, or interrupt a student's career,
emotional and mental illnesses play an important role.

Dr Ryle is well qualified to discuss the nature and causes of
student ill-health. He had several years' experience in general
practice, showing a particular interest in the incidence of
psychiatric disorders, before assuming charge of the student
health service in the University of Sussex. He writes not only
as a doctor, and a scientist, but also as a person who is still
young enough to sympathize with the predicaments and the
emotional turmoils of those students who are unlucky enough
to run into serious difficulties. At the same time, he shows a
lively concern not merely to deal with student casualties, but to
show how they occur, and how they may be prevented. His
book can be commended both to students, and to those of
their teachers who like to take an informed interest in student
welfare in its widest sense.

G. M. CARSTAIRS

Preface

A growing proportion of young people is undergoing higher education and the purpose of this book is to examine their academic and psychological experience. The central focus is upon students; who they are, what are the main emotional problems they have to face, what sort of human difficulties underlie their breaking down, dropping out or failing, and what kind of meaning is to be attached to their various non-conformist behaviours? Students are members of a particular society with particular demands to cope with and conditions to fulfil and their individual problems can only be fully understood in the context of this society. They are people growing up and learning, not raw materials being processed. As well as describing the students' problems, therefore, I have attempted to suggest ways in which the teaching methods and culture of the university may either contribute to, or alleviate, the problems of the individual student. The central thesis here is that the student casualty lists provide a measure of the quality of the university's life just as much as they indicate the vulnerability of the students.

It is hoped that the book may help those students who find themselves or their friends in difficulty, and also the tutors to whom the student so often presents his problems. It may also play a small part in informing and persuading all those involved in the development of our system of higher education.

In writing this book I have inevitably drawn heavily upon my own experience of setting up a health service in a new, rapidly expanding university, and I would like to acknowledge my considerable good fortune in finding such open-minded and co-operative colleagues on the faculty at the University of Sussex. I would also like to say how much the growth of my ideas has depended upon my continuing discussions with Dr Shadforth, Dr Gough, Dr Payne and Dr Tabor, my colleagues in this university health service. Dr Nicholas Malleson deserves credit for persuading the University of Sussex to plan for a comprehensive service from the beginning and, more generally, for being one of the first voices raised in Britain in favour of a wider concept of university medicine. I am of course indebted to the numerous other colleagues, known personally or through their writings, who have laid the foundations upon which present student health practice is based. Finally, I am grateful to Mrs Marion Higgins for her secretarial services in preparing the manuscript.

I have talked throughout in terms of universities, because this is the limit of my own experience, but with minor modifications the points made are relevant to any institution of higher education, and in a more general way, the principles discussed could be applied in many other contexts.

1   Introduction

The modern student, as represented in newspapers and on television, is long-haired, unwashed, pot-smoking, promiscuous and protesting. Each item in this composite portrait reflects a facet of reality but the whole is a distortion. The most characteristic activity of the student is to study – universities see to that – but this, and the less exotic manifestations of growing up, are not newsworthy. And yet these tasks of growing up and of acquiring the mental skills which will make students respected and valuable citizens in the future are central to their experience. These tasks are, however, not always completed, or, if they are, often not without cost. This book is mostly about the casualties – those who break down in health, fail at their work, or drop out of university. It should be noted at the outset that, despite their own immaturity, most students thread their ways through the maze of conflicting demands and pressures of life at university, often inadequately supplied with support or advice, and emerge at the other end with something gained, including a degree. Even many of those who at some stage are numbered among the fallen recover and eventually reap the rewards of a completed course and a completed phase in their lives. It is important, therefore, to remember human resilience.

Many survive but not all. How many fail or are injured on the way is not always apparent and one task of this book is to describe the student population and to provide some estimate of the size and nature of the casualty lists. Another task is to discuss these casualties in ways which can help tutors to recognize signs of trouble and help students themselves understand their own and their friends' problems. A further task is to investigate the causes of difficulty and to weigh up how far these date back to events occurring before the university, how far they reflect the effect of the university itself and how far they can be remedied. This examination of the relation between the university and the failure or breakdown of the student will involve touching upon some of the wider issues relating psychiatry to teaching and to the functioning of psychiatrists in the university setting.

Before we count the casualties, we must define them. Two main types of difficulty are under consideration – on the one hand emotional problems and mental illness; on the other hand academic failure. As regards emotional and mental problems, the decisions as to what level of disturbance is pathological is to some extent arbitrary and operational definitions must be provided. Not every student who is anxious or depressed, or who behaves irrationally, or who has doubts about his future, or problems over motivation, is to be regarded as a psychiatric casualty. To commit some follies and suffer some distresses is a normal part of growing up (and, indeed, of being grown up) and it is only when the deviation is extreme or when the conflicts are re-enacted repeatedly, without resolution, or when they interfere seriously with the individual's intentions and projects, that one need think in terms of pathology. In the student age-group in particular, evidence of what constitutes disorder or difficulty must always be considered in relation to the psychological tasks involved in the transition from adolescence into adulthood.

Criteria of academic difficulty are in general easier to establish. Here, the casualties are those students who are seen to perform below capacity, those who fail to reach the standard demanded by the university and those who fail to get the degrees for which they have been studying, whether by dropping out of university, being sent down, or by failing their examinations.

There is obviously a considerable overlap in the casualty lists defined by these two sets of criteria and one of the main concerns of the book will be to study, in detail, the interaction between academic progress and psychological disorder.

But how far are the problems of students specific to their occupation and how far simply a function of their age? To answer this we must consider the student population from which the casualties are drawn, and note the ways in which this population differs from the population as a whole.

THE STUDENT IN THE MODERN WORLD

Before proceeding with the detailed study of these questions some examination of contemporary student life is called for. Clearly the experience is very different from what it was one or two generations ago. In the older universities, scholars may still be distinguished from gentlemen – a distinction which, historically, implied more respect for breeding than for learning – but today's gentlemen must be scholarly too. Elegant and cultivated discourse may still flourish, but the stone quadrangles and red-brick façades are more permeable than ever before to the noise of the outside world. Academic excellence may still be prized, but increasingly it has to be seen as relevant to a society which grows in complexity at a staggering rate and which needs more and more people capable of exercising highly developed abilities and skills. The modern student is not to be regarded any more simply as enjoying a privileged retreat from the harsh reality of the world; he is developing, through his education, society's most precious asset. Older generations may look upon his activities with incomprehension, disapproval or envy but the student himself cannot escape an awareness of his value and he is increasingly insistent upon appropriate recognition and rights.

Our society has recognized its need for more graduates by enlarging, over the past decade, our higher educational facilities, particularly in the field of science and technology; ironically, this rather belated move has been paralleled by a trend among young people away from natural science (despite the security of career which is offered) towards the human sciences and the arts. This trend, I believe, can be seen as part of a larger movement – a movement expressed in new attitudes to politics and to personal relationships, to new forms of sexual behaviour and, less hopefully, to the cults of drug-taking and dropping-out. The apparent certainties of science and the control over nature that these give are seen as less satisfying than the attempt to understand human problems and to explore experience and feeling; an attitude summarized in 1968 by the French students with slogans such as *'l'imagination au pouvoir'*.

The instability of the modern world, and a felt revulsion against its violence and injustices, make it difficult for many contemporary students to identify with any stable system of belief; at a time when the demands made by society are more and more complicated, the relation of the individual to society is becoming more cautious and less committed. These factors lie rather outside the scope of this book, but they form a back-cloth to the smaller stage upon which the student's personal themes of growing and learning are played out. It is a backcloth above all of uncertainty, and it is not surprising that this uncertainty is reflected especially clearly in the thoughts, feelings and actions of an age-group primarily concerned with the search for personal identity.

2   The University – Who Gets There and What Do They Find?

University students in Britain represent only seven to eight per cent of their age-group. How is this *élite* selected?

THE POOL OF TALENT – SECONDARY EDUCATION

Nowadays getting a university place depends upon getting good 'A' level results and, for the majority who are educated in State schools, this is only possible for those who get into a comprehensive or grammar school at the 11-plus selection. Passing the 11-plus itself means that the individual must have developed fast enough and must have had the appropriate type of temperament to have been taught in one of the higher primary school streams.

This rigid school system, unique to Britain, has been apparently successful in selecting out suitable university candidates. 'Apparently', however, is a key word in this sentence. The predictions made at selection were essentially self-fulfilling; the pupil who failed at any stage of the selection process had very little chance of re-entering the university-bound segment of the school population, even if his intelligence were equivalent and his personality resilient enough to maintain morale in the face of being defined as a failure. The effect of this system of selection has been to cut down the number of applicants for each university place, an effect which in the past has been justified by theories which asserted that the pool of ability was strictly limited so that university expansion could only lead to a lowering of the standard of student accepted ('more means worse').

There are many convincing arguments against this concept of a narrowly limited pool of ability and many of the assumptions have now been rejected;[19, 24, 60] as a result, the more absurd rigidities of this system are now at long last being modified, especially by the development of the comprehensive schools.

In the past the system must have led to the exclusion from universities of many individuals of potential talent. Those who do survive all the hurdles and reach university must be a selected group. What sort of background do they come from and what type of personality are they likely to display?

Selection by Performance

Many intelligent school children must be lost from the academic stream but few unintelligent ones survive in it and this, coupled with the modest proportion of the population (by international standards), reaching university in Britain means that intellectual inadequacy is seldom a cause of failure or of stress in British university students. It may well be, however, that the type of intelligence favoured by our selection system is restricted. In particular, it tends to overvalue convergent thinking (the sort which is good at finding answers, but bad at inventing questions) and hence may exclude potentially creative students in favour of some less original. Hudson[26] has shown that the mode or style of thinking is extremely influential in the schoolboy's choice of arts or science in the fifth form, those who choose science tending to be convergent thinkers, and those who choose arts to be divergent thinkers. This polarization may be understandable in terms of interests and subject matter, but may not be entirely desirable from the point of view of either arts or sciences, as those whose thinking involves a blend or balance of styles may well prove to be the more original and productive in either field. Elsewhere Hudson[27] has argued that the narrowing down of criteria and the greater emphasis upon formal measures, such as 'A' level results, which have accompanied the democratization of university entrance in Britain, may have led to an overvaluation of the unoriginal. Not every type of ability can be measured by competence at examination performance over a range of three subjects, indeed some who excel at this may prove ill at ease when faced with the more unstructured intellectual demands of a university.

Selection by Temperament

The competitive pressure and the narrow criteria of success at school mean that survival through to the stage of further education calls for ambition and also for a high degree of conformity and compliance. The original thinker of rebellious temperament may well give up or be excluded. On the other hand, the successful, compliant schoolboy or schoolgirl, once at university and faced with the increased demand and opportunity for independence can soon be transformed into a failing, frustrated or defiant undergraduate. This reaction of the previously conformist, which may be manifest in academic failure, leaving university, protest politics or neurosis, accounts, I believe, for a significant proportion of student casualties. The family background that favours academic success may tend to provoke this type of reaction, for the mother who rears high-achieving children is often more authoritarian and restrictive than is the mother of the cheerful plodder,[14] and the family which accords acceptance conditionally in return for achievement may breed, as well as Fellows of the Royal Society, drop-outs and revolutionaries.

Selection for Emotional Health

From the above, it is clear that some of those who reach university will have a need to revolt against the combined pressures which helped to carry them there, and this need may be expressed through neurotic, compulsive behaviour. Apart from these, however, university entrants are likely to be more stable than their peers. There is clear evidence[13] that children who show aggressive, delinquent or neurotic traits at school, most of whom come from disturbed home backgrounds, are unlikely to realize their full intellectual potential. For this reason the university population, selected for intellectual achievement, must also be selected to a considerable extent for psychological health. Looking at the range of emotional problems encountered among students, one can only murmur, 'God help the others.'

Selection by Social Class

Another factor of major importance in selection for university education in Britain is social class. Even if one ignores the influence of the private schools, the child from a lower social class is at a disadvantage educationally when compared to his fellows of equivalent intelligence. This disadvantage is less apparent at an early age but grows rapidly from twelve onwards. Our school system fails to make use of much potential talent and three in four children intellectually able to continue leave school at the first opportunity. This may be due to the tenuous hold in the minds of many working-class children of those middle-class values which make achievement and success such desired qualities; and in particular there may be a greater reluctance among working-class adolescents to prolong either financial or psychological dependency. The poorer standard of State schools in working-class areas and the relative lack of stimulation in many working-class families may also play a part. For whatever reason, a far lower proportion of working-class children will reach university than is the case for middle-class children of the same intellectual level. The working-class student may therefore be expected to show, to an exaggerated degree, the qualities associated with selection in general, needing stronger motivation and higher intelligence to overcome the obstacles.

ROLE CONFLICTS IN UNIVERSITY WOMEN

One other factor in selection remains to be discussed: the particular position of women. Equal opportunities for higher education for women are relatively recent and incomplete, and, in the culture as a whole, a woman's concern for achievement and for a career is still often seen as conflicting with her role as woman, that is to say as wife and mother. In consequence the female student may face a conflict, unknown to her male contemporaries, between her sexual identity and her student identity. Superficially, this may be reflected in ploys like 'playing dumb' so as not to scare the boys away. More fundamentally, it can be a factor of real significance in determining her motivation. Among girls selected for university places, there will be some who accept a career as a natural right, but others in whom ambition constitutes a form of 'masculine protest'; such girls are likely to have underlying sex role conflicts. Conversely, the woman who is feminine in the more traditional sense may be more preoccupied with forming relationships than with graduation. Work for her may seem, at times, remote and irrelevant to the central projects of her life and the pressure to achieve may represent an assault upon her central concerns and values. Experimental studies[21, 22] have demonstrated that more feminine girls, showing more positive identification with warm mothers, tend to do relatively poorly at academic work. More anecdotally, it is not uncommon for the girl who is depressed or in academic difficulty to abandon her books and retreat into a domestic phase in which she feeds her friends, makes clothes or refurbishes her living-room, putting all thoughts of literary criticism or physics firmly out of her mind.

THE IMPACT OF THE UNIVERSITY

For most highly-achieving boys and girls university has long been represented as a point on the horizon towards which to strive. The desirability of the goal is unquestioned, and, on arrival, expectations are high. The experience itself is likely to prove something of a shock, provoking both disappointment and anxiety. The disappointment will find its focus on a variety of targets, from the simple problems of indifferent food and lodgings to the lack of elegance and clarity in the teaching. Basically this is a disappointment at finding that the world here is no less imperfect than elsewhere, whatever the glossy brochures seem to promise, and this disappointment can, if extreme, represent a recapitulation of early deprivations and conflicts. The anxiety experienced by the new student will probably spring from his uncertainty of status in the transition from being a big fish in the school pond to being a small, lost fish in the university sea. The insecure majority see their fellow students, on first inspection, as clever and original to a man. The student on arrival has few sources of acceptance other than those which he achieves by his own efforts. He is moving away from the role of son or daughter and the self-evident acceptance provided by a satisfactory family. His contemporaries, bound to him by no established tie or contract, are the shifting mirror in which he tries to define himself. This complex and competitive situation can allow rapid growth and development in those with adequately firm inner resources, but for others, particularly for those with disturbed family backgrounds and unresolved conflicts, the situation is dangerous.

In the early weeks reassurance and confirmation of identity may be sought by a number of means. Acceptance may be won from fellow students by sociability, by eccentricity, by the fluent expression of the general disillusionment, by the setting up or joining of illicit sub-cultures, for example around drugs, or more generally, by the consolidation of in-groups and cliques. Approval may be won from tutors by the familiar means of achievement, but this may be inhibited by fears or fantasies of their elevated intelligence and status. To the isolated or shy, neither fellow students nor tutors may be approachable and to these the reassurance offered by the family or by friends at home may provide the only sure refuge, so that social initiative within the university may be blunted.

The lack of dependable sources of acceptance, the uncertainty of role and the possible conflict between roles, and the exposure to the challenge of an unstructured environment in which debate about values and an absence of imposed ideologies are prized, can all combine to provoke a sense of fragmentation and unreality in the student – the state of identity diffusion. The dangers of this may be less marked for the student who is embarking upon a professional career, for here his identity as a student is already linked with his long-term role in the wider society. For those doing less oriented courses there is no such anchor; and this group will include some who have chosen subjects without any direct career implication, precisely because they are uncertain about their own identity. For these, to some extent, the student years can be an evasion rather than a means of developing identity.

POSTPONING UNIVERSITY ENTRANCE

Some of the problems of this settling-in period might be avoided if the decision to go to university were more consciously and directly made. At present it is widely assumed that the clever sixth-former will take 'A' levels and apply for a university place, and only a minority of those who qualify for a place follow alternative careers, or even spend an intermediate year after leaving school before committing themselves to university. If entrance requirements were less rigid and if it were more feasible for students to come to university after a period at work, the pressure on those of uncertain motivation to take up a place on leaving school would diminish, and I suspect that fewer would regret or waste their opportunity.

STUDENT SUB-CULTURES

It would be an over-simplification to regard the student culture as a single or unchanging entity. At any one time different students in a given institution may operate in quite different groups and according to a diversity of values and at different times in the same institution the dominant attitudes and behaviour of students may show marked shifts. American sociological investigations of college peer groups have highlighted some of the dominant trends, and in particular have put forward a fourfold classification of student sub-cultures into the 'collegiate', the 'vocational', the 'academic' and the 'nonconformist'.[7]

The 'collegiate' sub-culture is characterized by a loyalty to the college which is expressed primarily through social and sporting activities, with academic commitment running a poor second. Students who operate predominantly in this culture are likely to be wealthy and not vocationally committed. One suspects that the English equivalent of this culture is small and diminishing under present-day competitive pressures.

The 'vocational' sub-culture is characterized by an approach which is narrowly practical and down to earth; the student is using the university as a means of ensuring his own upward social mobility, and is committed to it only in these terms.

The 'academic' sub-culture is made up of those seriously committed to education, beyond the confines of particular courses and degrees; these are students identified with the faculty and with the ideals of the academic world.

Finally, the 'non-conformist' student may share with the academic a concern for learning and a capacity for it, but his commitment to the college is less intense and, in so far as it exists, it is likely to be rebellious. This culture, in various forms, provides a social expression for adolescent rebellion – an expression which may, at times, appear futile or dangerous, but which also frequently acts as a leaven. Writing in 1969 one can see that the commitment of this student sub-culture to the wider society is not to be underestimated.

Not every student, of course, falls neatly into one of these categories; indeed any one individual may make a partial identification with the values of more than one. The relationship an individual makes with the university and with his fellow students is determined both by his own psychological needs and by the structure of the community in which he finds himself. The aim of a university must be to minimize conflict between its own values and those of its student cultures, and to ensure that these values in turn do not conflict with the psychological needs of a wide range of individual students.

The preliminary settling-in period may last through most of the first year and it is during this time that the majority of withdrawals from the university occur. By the end of this period the survivors, to varying degrees, have embarked upon a number of tasks; they have developed interests and extra-curricular activities and have sorted out congenial groups of fellow students; they have accepted a new independence from the family, they have begun to see themselves, in some form or other, in the student role, and, in some cases, to feel the connection between this role and their lifelong social and professional ambitions. They have begun to learn the difference between school and university work, developing a new initiative and independence. Many will have experienced relationships with the other sex which are more than an anxious testing out of their own sexual capacity. In all these ways they have been engaged in the transition from an adolescent to an adult status. The general problems of this transition, and the particular difficulties of students, are discussed in the next chapter.

3　Adolescent into Adult: Problems of Transition

In the last chapter we have seen how the student is an atypical member of his age-group: more intelligent than most, more ambitious to achieve, more likely to have problems of compliance and defiance, more likely, despite this, to be relatively emotionally stable. The social background is more likely to be middle-class and for the girl student there may well be a particular problem of combining the sex role with the student role. In a number of ways, these special characteristics and the nature of the university experience impose the form which problems take among students, but in essence the problems themselves are not very different from those of the age-group as a whole. Basically these are problems related to the completion of the task of growing up and of relinquishing dependence. One can, in our society, leave school at fifteen, commit rape at sixteen, drive a car at seventeen, vote at eighteen, and each of these new rights and responsibilities represents social recognition of a new status and performs, in a rather disjointed way, the functions of the more formal *rites de passage* of primitive societies. Clearly, in one sense, going to university can represent another such rite.

Before this transition from adolescent to adult status is embarked upon, the individual defines himself largely in terms of his role in the family on which he is economically and psychologically dependent. After it is complete, he sees himself in terms of his individual social roles defined by occupation, status and group membership, and in due course, in terms of the new family which he founds. This transformation occurs during years of rapid biological change, marked by the development of new strengths and the eruption of new and powerful drives. These are years in which inner forces and outer demands change with bewildering speed so that the individual's own body and his social role are both unfamiliar. The psychological task to be accomplished through all these changes is to preserve and develop a personal identity and a capacity to relate to others.

For the student the transition from school and home to university represents a particularly abrupt alteration in status. From a position of relative dependence upon and control by parents and teachers, he enters a community where supports and controls from authority figures are fewer and less powerful, and where, on the other hand, pressures from his contemporaries (all, like him, dealing with a new independence with a mixture of anxiety and exultation) can be extreme. Not surprisingly the most common problem encountered by the student relates to his identity. One can almost believe the story told of an American student, doubtless well versed in paperbacks, who consulted his university health service 'because he had not yet experienced his identity crisis and thought something must be wrong.'

If previous personality development has been reasonably smooth and if the social pressures are not too extreme the identity problems of this age-group will be coped with satisfactorily. Problems when they do arise will generally take the form of a re-enactment in the present situation of those conflicts not resolved at earlier stages. To some extent, this re-enactment is a normal aspect of adolescent behaviour. Erikson,[15] who has contributed much to the understanding of this phase, describes it in these words:

The growing and developing youths faced with this physiological revolution within them and with tangible adult tasks ahead of them are now primarily concerned with what they appear to be in the eyes of others, as compared with what they feel they are, and with the question of how to connect the roles and skills cultivated earlier with the occupational prototypes of the day. In their search for a new sense of continuity and sameness, adolescents have to refight many of the battles of earlier years, even though to do so they must artificially appoint perfectly well-meaning people to play the roles of adversaries; and they are ever ready to instal lasting idols and ideals as guardians of a final identity. . . . The danger of this stage is role confusion. Where this is based on a strong previous doubt as to one's identity, delinquent and outright psychotic episodes are not uncommon.

Who will fail and who will succeed in the transition? No parents can hope to respond appropriately to the emergence of each new capacity in their children and in every parent/child relationship there are bound to be conflicts. Most people with serious emotional problems, however, come from families in which these conflicts are exacerbated by the absence of a parent, by discord between the parents, or by the emotional problems of the parents. It is the addition of these difficulties to the normal problems of growing up which can make the individual vulnerable through all the subsequent stages of his life.

PERSONALITY DEVELOPMENT

To give an account of personality development in a few pages is not easy and what follows is bound to be over-condensed. It represents an attempt to analyse the forces which go to shape the adult personality. These forces are of two main sorts – biological and cultural. It is my intention to describe the interaction of these forces, paying particular attention to the issues of importance during the transition from adolescence to adulthood.

Genetic Influences

That genetic factors are important is a matter of common observation. On the one hand detailed family resemblances in personality are often present to a degree which it is hard to explain on any other basis, and twin studies, including those on identical twins separately reared, confirm this everyday observation. On the other hand, children of the same parents reared in the same home are often absurdly different – and here longitudinal studies from infancy onwards confirm that basic differ-ences (for example in responsiveness to new experience, in tendency to explore the environment and in tolerance of frustration) are indeed present from the time of birth. For this reason it is impossible to establish the exact weight to be attached to genetic factors in determining personality, for each child from birth will behave differently towards his parents and others around him, and will hence elicit different responses.

Cultural Influences – The Family

The importance of nurture as well as nature is attested by numerous cross-cultural studies, by experimental studies on animals, and it is of course a basic assumption in psycho-analysis. Psychoanalytic theory, developing on the basis of work with adults, first explored this field through the fantasies, regressions and memories of adult patients. Developmental studies of infants have only latterly been considered. The classical formulations of the stages of infantile development into oral, anal and genital (redefined by Erikson as, respectively, stages of trust versus mistrust, autonomy versus shame and doubt, and initiative versus guilt) still lack confirmation from developmental studies; patients in analytic treatment, however, persist in producing material which seems explicable in these terms. The most important contribution made by Freud, how-ever, may well be that he emphasized the fact that adult per-sonality is the result of a process of development; his own model of this development, even in its successive modifications, may still prove inaccurate and in need of clearer formulation before it is capable of proof or disproof.

The culture to which the developing child is exposed is a changing one, responding all the time to his own growth and development. Initially, the infant is helpless and entirely de-pendent, and the central person in his life is bound to be the mother (or her substitute) who holds and feeds him. It is in relation to this mother, therefore, that the child has his first experience of the self as distinct from another, and his first experience of another as being available, giving comfort and food, and yet as being capable also of going away and depriving him of the comfort demanded. With further growth, the child becomes more active in this relationship, being increasingly able, through the second and third years of life, to make his needs and frustrations known, and being now able to defy the mother by rejecting her food, refusing to accept her pot training, and through making independent attempts to explore his environment with his own still very limited motor powers, even when this means going against his mother's wishes. With this further development, the father, and perhaps the siblings, play an increasing part in the child's life – a part combining support with threat. Rivalry and competition become important issues, sharpening the child's sense of his own individuality and exposing him to more people who can both help and frustrate him. In so far as these others are competitors for the mother on whom he is most dependent, he has to deal with his fear and anger in relation to them. In the case of boys, this rivalry with the father forms the kernel of the Oedipus complex, to be resolved between the ages of three and five by identification with the father and the taking on of a new, independent male identity. In the case of girls, the analogous process consists of settling for a new relationship with the father which offers some of the advantages of the mother's role. Non-analytical evidence has not confirmed all the details of this process, but does point to the crucial role of the father's differential response to sons and daughters as determining the child's sense of sexual identity. Parallel to the acquisition of this identity, the child's behaviour becomes less dependent upon the rewards and punishments meted out by the parents, and more determined by inner controls, notably guilt, derived from an internalization of the parental values.

The details of the above account are by no means universally accepted and there is still much controversy between different schools of psychoanalysis. Unambiguous evidence linking specific parental behaviour at particular stages of infantile development with subsequent clear-cut deviations of personality is lacking. Such links would be hard to prove conclusively if only because parental behaviour is itself a function of parental personality and hence is likely to be a constant factor through all stages of the child's development. The psychoanalytic use of terms with developmental connotations as descriptions of personality (e.g. oral-dependent or anal-sadistic) is perhaps confusing in view of the absence of firmer evidence.

It does, however, seem reasonable and useful to assume that the child's experience of its mother, father and siblings is likely to be critical in forming his conception of what is possible in his relationships with others, so that later on in life his relationships with women, men, those in authority, those in competition and so on, will be heavily influenced by this first experience. Even though development may be less predetermined by early experience than classical psychoanalytic theory would suggest, the individual's capacity to be related yet separate, to trust others, while accepting the limitations of what they can offer, to be autonomous, yet be able to concede some power and control to others, to feel secure in his sex role, and to take on responsibility for his own behaviour must surely be derived in large part from this early family experience.

Adolescence

The early development of the child occurs on a background of rapid biological growth; in the later years of childhood the pace slows down, and psychological conflicts are also, for a time, less prominent. At puberty there is a spurt in growth, accompanied by rapid gains in most capacities and by the emergence of sexual drives. These rapid changes call for intense social and psychological adjustments and are inevitably accompanied by some degree of conflict.

In the most general terms, adolescents are faced with the problem of their own identity. Before the transition, this is largely determined for them by their family role and, to some degree, by their role in their peer group culture in society at large or at school. After the transition, they must be able to see themselves as independent men or women, pursuing some occupational goal and preparing themselves for the future role of husband or wife and parent. During the transition, they have to deal with the problem of separating from their parents and family, of establishing their own relationships with others, of accepting the limitations of such relationships. They have to come to terms with their need to accept authority, while refusing to concede too much, and they have to test out and confirm their sexual identity. In all these ways, they are recapitulating in new guises the sorts of problem which they have to face first during infancy.

Neurotic Problems of Adolescence – The neurotic problems of this age-group (and of later ones) are based upon failure in one of the developmental tasks – a failure which has left the individual restricted in some way in his relation to others. In most cases the problem is not so much that earlier experiences have left the neurotic individual with an irredeemable lack or with an incurable wound, as that they have equipped him with a set of assumptions about himself and other people which apparently limit the range of ways open to him for relating to others. If a man has never fully detached himself from his mother, his relationship with women may be dominated by the attempt to repeat, or by the need to escape a repetition of this pattern. If childhood is recalled as a time of deprivation and rejection, others may be seized upon as potential sources of milk and honey, or attacked for their failure to be such paragons, the type of behaviour which one can relate to the infant's experience of the 'two-faced breast'. If the struggle for power with the parents was bitter and prolonged, relationships with authority figures may be similarly bitter, marked either by resentful compliance or by passive resistance, while in relationships with weaker people the pattern of the parents' domination may be recapitulated. In these and many other ways, the individual with a neurotic personality seeks out others who will play the familiar games, dictates the terms of his interaction with them and fails to observe those attributes of the other which contradict his basic assumptions. Though the resulting experience of others is usually frustrating and painful, the neurotic, who has 'learned not to learn' clings to his limited construction of the world as if it was an essential part of himself. Only through the experience of others who refuse to collude with this restricted and restricting structure can he escape from the defences which imprison him.

STUDENT IDENTITY AT UNIVERSITY

The transitions of adolescence are always rapid but for the student entering the university they are abrupt. Under these circumstances it is not surprising that identity problems commonly occur, and, in these, tutors are particularly liable to be appointed 'to play the role of adversaries' or other roles, which repeat or complement those experienced or fantasized by the student in his relationship with his parents. The psychoanalytically-minded observer can see, in some of these conflicts, symbolizations of the infantile conflicts, for teaching, like feeding, can be emphatically 'spat out', and the call for a weekly essay can echo earlier regular demands. These parallels will seem fanciful to many, but one student at least (perhaps to be obliging) produced evidence for such an association. This student was in treatment for a work problem, being quite unable to produce his weekly essay, and he dreamt that his tutor had an infant on his knee to which he was giving an enema 'to ensure the production of regular motions'. Such direct symbolization is of course rare, but an understanding of the themes outlined above can be of help in making sense of otherwise inexplicable and irrational behaviour.

Later chapters will discuss the various courses of work difficulty and give examples of some of these processes – meanwhile, one can say that whenever the resolution of childhood conflicts is incomplete the reality of the relationship of the student with his tutor and with the institution can become distorted.

THE EFFECT OF THE UNIVERSITY

Granted that a university must foster independence, make demands and measure the capacity of its students, and to this extent can all too easily be cast by the neurotic into the role of a depriving, demanding or threatening parent, how far can it avoid provoking disturbance in more vulnerable students? The attempt to answer this question is one of the tasks of this book, but hard evidence is not plentiful. It seems best, therefore, to make clear at the outset my personal conclusion that, while there is bound to be an irreducible minimum of casualties, high rates of personal breakdown and of academic failure should make one suspect that the practices of the university should be a matter for observation and concern.[53]

How far an institution elicits neurotic responses from its students depends, I believe, upon its atmosphere and its mode of operation. If it offers cues too reminiscent of common childhood difficulties, if, to offer an over-simple analogy, the university is like a disturbed family, then it is more likely that the re-enactment of old conflicts will dominate the student's behaviour and block personal growth and academic progress. If, on the other hand, it can provide a reasonable, concerned and flexible environment, if its demands and pressures are balanced by supports, if continuing attention is paid to the student's views and feelings, then it is likely that the student, even if vulnerable, will be able to use his university years to further his own development and to pursue his academic aims.

4   How Many Fall Ill?

The classification of an individual as sick rather than well, lazy, stupid or sinful, will vary greatly with the values of the culture and with the availability and orientation of the doctors. Reported rates of mental and emotional illness in a community, especially illness of the milder varieties, will therefore depend as much upon the availability of services and the attitudes towards psychiatry as upon the 'real' prevalence of disorder.

With this preamble it will be clear that figures about prevalence need to be interpreted with some caution. It is therefore surprising to discover that universities in both Britain and North America, and over a long period in the latter country, report pretty consistent rates of psychiatric illness wherever there is a service capable of assessing, treating, and hence counting, the cases. Figures given below are within the range reported by the great majority of published surveys.[1, 12, 17, 31, 32, 50, 57, 58]

INCIDENCE OF PSYCHIATRIC DISORDER

Severe Cases

Over a three- to four-year undergraduate course between one and two per cent of students will experience severe psychiatric illness of a type requiring hospital admission. The majority of this group will be suffering from psychotic illness, some with schizophrenia, some with affective psychoses (manic-depression), and some with schizophrenia-like illnesses labelled

schizo-affective disorders which, though florid, carry a better
chance for full recovery than does schizophrenia itself.

Moderate Cases

A further ten to twenty per cent of the student population will
present, at some stage, with an emotional or psychological
problem sufficient to need some treatment. Of this group, about
one-third suffer from relatively serious neurotic and personality
disorders, typically related to late adolescent identity crises.
This group may well need relatively prolonged psychotherapy.
The remainder are milder cases, perhaps needing support over
crises or brief psychotherapy or counselling.

Milder Cases

Approximately a further twenty per cent of the student body
will report transient psychological or psychosomatic symptoms,
representing reactions to the normal stresses of their age and
environment and requiring no more than reassurance and
perhaps brief medication. This group will include many of the
well-known pre-examination stress reactions.

Rates Measured by Questionnaires

The above figures are derived from cases presenting to clinical
services. Surveys involving whole populations, using question-
naires or symptom inventories, tend to indicate higher rates of
disturbance (though here again the definition of abnormality is
arbitrary). There are many individuals with abnormal scores
on personality inventories who apparently function quite satisfactorily, though with observation over longer periods it is
likely that, eventually, a fairly high proportion of these will
become ill.

Rates in Non-Students

It is impossible to say whether these rates for students are
different from the rates in the age-group as a whole, because

the provision of psychiatric facilities for adolescents outside universities is lamentably sparse, and hence comparable opportunities to record such rates are lacking. Students might tend to have lower rates, as emotional disturbance is associated with poor school achievement, or a higher rate due to the stresses of the university. In the general population just over two per cent of this age-group are hospitalized each year for psychiatric illness,[4] so the student rate, of one or two per cent over three years, is lower. Apart from the effect of pre-selection, social class factors and better out-patient or on-campus facilities for the early treatment of students may account for this. The proportion of the population in the student age-range consulting each year with neurosis, as recorded in general practice studies, runs at between five and fifteen per cent, the rates for women being one-and-a-half times to twice the rates for men.[30, 48]

On balance, therefore, it looks as if students are more likely to consult than others, even though they are less likely to end up in hospital. One can postulate three possible explanations for this. Firstly, the late adolescent may be suspicious of the family general practitioner, his attitudes being derived from childhood, in which the doctor was seen as being allied to the parents. The mode of operation and reputation of a university health service, on the other hand, is likely to encourage consultation, for in this setting the doctor is often seen as the ally of the student, as opposed to the quasi-parental role of the tutor. Secondly, while minor impairment of functioning due to emotional problems may be borne in many routine jobs without difficulty, it may be critical in the student who has major intellectual tasks to complete. Consultation, either at the student's or his tutor's request, is hence more likely to occur. Thirdly, rates of consultation for neurosis rise steeply with age in the general population in the late twenties and thirties. It seems possible that many of these cases have experienced difficulties to some degree earlier in their lives but have not sought treatment due to the inaccessibility or absence of facilities. Students, on the other hand, will often have such facilities available.

SEX AND FACULTY DIFFERENCES

Relatively few reports on the rates of psychiatric illness in universities give any analysis of their figures by sex and faculty. It is generally agreed that the rate among women is some one-and-a-half to twice times as high as among men; as mentioned above this finding is common to all adult age-groups where psychiatric disorder is concerned, and therefore is unlikely to be a specific effect of the university environment. As regards faculty differences, there is general agreement in both published and anecdotal evidence that students of fine arts and literature are most prone to consult, while students of pure and applied sciences are least prone. At Sussex University we have found that psychiatric illness is more common in arts students than in science students, and more common in women than in men.[50]

How far these differences represent an effect of recruitment and how far they reflect differences in the demands and pressures of different courses remains uncertain. There are aspects of science teaching which could be supportive; for example, the teaching is more structured and there are more group activities than on the arts side. In addition, it may be that attitudes towards psychiatry differ between the faculties. Scientists are more often cautious about human relationships and are more likely to show an intolerance of human weakness which could make them reluctant to consult. Arts students, on the other hand, place more value on feeling and on relationships and are more prepared to accept a degree of neuroticism in view of its assumed relationship with creativity. Attitudes to consultation could not account for all the differences, however. Personality measures of arts and science students taken before or on arrival at the university already contrast markedly, which suggests that the fairly protracted process of academic selection may account for much of the observed difference in illness rates. Testing students on arrival at Sussex University with the Eysenck Personality Inventory,[16] for example, we found a significantly higher average neuroticism score for male arts students compared to male science students. Other differences – for example, in convergent/divergent thinking patterns – have been shown to be of importance by Hudson,[26] and much other evidence and common observation goes to suggest that in many ways students in different faculties are different kinds of animals. One should be careful before blaming the subject or the environment of a particular department for the level of the disturbance found in the students working in it.

THE PREDICTION OF BREAKDOWN

It would clearly be of value if the student vulnerable to breakdown could be detected early in his career but this is only possible to a limited extent.

A self-report of symptoms, obtainable by using various types of symptom-questionnaire or personality inventory, will enable one to pick out a sample of students with high scores. The group will, over the three ensuing years, have a disproportionate share of psychiatric trouble. All such tests, however, involve a high percentage of misclassification, which is to say that many who later become patients will have scored in the normal score range and many high scorers will survive without the benefit of psychiatry. Relatively few other accessible data have been shown to be related to subsequent psychiatric status. Kidd,[31] in a cohort study at Edinburgh, investigated the relationship of a large number of factors (family background, social class, medical history, etc.) to subsequent psychiatric illness. Students reporting symptoms on arrival or giving a history of previous illness or consultation were more likely to consult with psychiatric illness. Apart from these, men neither of whose parents were graduates and men not following in their parents' profession were more prone to subsequent psychiatric illness. Not having been an 'all-rounder' at school and not having been a participator in social clubs was associated in both men and women with subsequent psychiatric illness. Kidd also found, as have others, significantly higher rates of psychiatric breakdown among overseas students coming from non-Western cultures. In another study, 100 psychiatric student patients at Oxford were assessed when they were referred to the psychiatrist.[11]

They were compared with 100 volunteer controls and a previous personal or family history of psychiatric disorder was found to be significantly more common in the patient group. The patients were also more likely to have abnormal scores on a personality inventory. By combining a classification by the score on the inventory with somato-typing (a classification of body-build which has a relationship to liability to some sorts of psychiatric illness) patients could be separated from controls with only about twenty per cent ending up in the wrong category. However, it is by no means certain that the inventory scores would have been such effective discriminators if the tests had been completed earlier, before the illness.

SELECTION ON PSYCHIATRIC GROUNDS

A fairly common response to statements reporting the high rate of psychiatric illness in students is to suggest that better selection might eliminate these weak students, or alternatively that it might often be best to encourage them to leave university once they have presented. Does the evidence for a (rather feeble) predictive power imply that medical screening should be a part of normal selection procedures, and would a subsequent exclusion of the psychiatrically ill be justifiable? Personally, I think not. Technical limitations in this respect need to be emphasized. Neither medicine nor psychology can help us to predict high achievement, except to underwrite the obvious observation that people who tend to do well, tend to do well. Psychological testing may be able to detect intellectual potential in individuals showing poor performance, and psychiatry may be able to release such potential, but few such cases will reach selection committees for university entrance. The best that doctors can do is to predict high risk for certain individuals, and students who are being considered for admission who have a history suggesting such risk should, in their own and in the universities' interests, be medically screened. In the case of the applicant who has had a severe, especially a psychotic, illness, both the diagnosis and the duration and the quality of recovery need to be known; and in general a clear year since a major breakdown is advisable before starting on a university course. For candidates with a history of less serious disorder, medical screening may sometimes be advisable, provided the candidate gives permission. In such cases it may be unwise to admit without medical advice, but it is certainly unfair for laymen to exclude an applicant on 'psychiatric' grounds, in the absence of such advice – a not uncommon unfairness, I suspect.

Large-scale psychiatric screening, even if the methods available were effective, would have a number of bad effects. For one thing, the more importance a university placed upon 'good emotional health' in its applicants the more likely it would be that candidates and schools would falsify and suppress any history of difficulty. Even in strict academic terms, caution must be exercised – a view reinforced by Hudson's amusing paper[25] in which he described the likely outcome were the neurotic Darwin or the eccentric Einstein to apply today for post-graduate grants.

Even if our predictive skills were more highly developed, there are more general grounds for challenging the idea that the psychiatrically vulnerable student should be excluded at selection or weeded out on first presentation. The great majority of psychiatrically disturbed students are capable of reaching degree standard. If the performance of some is below their intellectual potential, others achieve highly because of neurotic drives. For many of these individuals psychiatric difficulty is a transient phase which will not dog them throughout their lives. In any case, the university should surely be more civilized than the general community and should show a greater willingness to contain people who deviate from the social norms, provided they meet academic requirements. Individuals who contrast their own stability with a neurotic's weakness may do so as a means of attempting to reassure themselves. Institutions which seek to exclude deviants may similarly be harbouring a blindness or intolerance far more destructive than any effect to be feared from the presence of neurotic people. Finally, only by admitting the vulnerable can the university come to terms with its own capacity to be damaging. In accommodating neurotics and in making provisions to meet their needs, the university has to assess its own contribution to their stability or to their break-down – an assessment which is likely to have good effects beyond those manifest in reducing overt illness.

Given that the prediction of psychiatric illness is to some degree possible, one could use predictive methods to develop some scheme of prophylactic intervention, offering help to the potentially ill student before he actually breaks down. To my knowledge, this idea has been voiced by many but carried out by none, due, I suspect, to the fact that health services, however lavish, tend to have more than enough clinical work to do without drumming up trade in this way. Even if such support were offered it would only provide a partial cover. The critical need, in my view, is to build up a system of easy access and of access by various routes, so that students, tutors and others, once alerted to the signs of trouble, however manifest, are able to seek prompt help for it.

In later chapters the bare figures presented in this section will be clothed with descriptions and case histories of various common types of student psychiatric problems. Meanwhile, the next chapter will focus upon the academic casualties and on the relation of psychiatric illness to university wastage and under-achievement.

5   Who Fails and Why?

The academic casualty list is made up of those who fail to reach their own or the university's standard, or who leave the course due to their own choice or the university's decision. The classification of these casualties can be made under four headings, as follows:

1. *Drop-outs – students leaving university permanently without obtaining a degree.*
2. *Interrupters – students taking time off from their course for some non-academic reason, but eventually returning.*
3. *Academic Problem Group – students identified as underachieving or in difficulty in the course of their studies.*
4. *Failures – students who fail to graduate, including those in groups 2 and 3 and students not previously identified as being in difficulty.*

How many students fall into each of these categories will depend on the policies and methods of the university in respect of selection, teaching and the right to readmission. Group 3, in particular, will only be identified if the university is on the look-out for them. *Which* individuals from the total student body become casualties will be determined by social, personal and intellectual factors. The relative importance of the various influences is difficult to disentangle, but what evidence does exist will now be reviewed, taking the four groups defined above separately.

DROP-OUTS

There are very large differences in drop-out rates between
different institutions and counties. American figures[8], [17], [23], [58]
are in general far higher than British ones,[38], [39], [50] often ex-
ceeding fifty per cent. This difference reflects, of course, a
difference in selection methods, in the number of available
places and, to some extent, in educational philosophy. The
British student has competed for his university place far more
fiercely than has his American counterpart and he may be expected to be that much more highly motivated and highly
selected. In the United States the student who drops out has a
much higher chance of gaining readmission to the same or
another university than does his English counterpart, who is apt
to find that the rule of no second chances, which began to
operate at his 11-plus selection, still applies.

In this context, most British universities aim to minimize
drop-out rates, although some departments reckon to fail a
considerable proportion of students after the first year of their
course. In my opinion, a 'weed out' policy like this has little
justification in human or economic terms, when one considers
the degree of pre-selection possible for the university and the
relative difficulty for the student of obtaining alternative higher
education. At the very least, such a policy of weeding out needs
to be combined with the provision of a service to help students
find alternative placements.

Universities which adopt the goal of getting every accepted
student through to Finals will still experience a loss of over five
per cent of their intake, mostly during the first year. Clearly
some of this loss represents the influence of rational choice and
change of mind about careers, but much of it represents the
effect of emotional and irrational factors.

Influence of the University

Because some students will survive any form of teaching and
because some students are palpably brighter than others, it is
always tempting to assume that the drop-out is a defective

student, and hence the only error committed by the university was in selection. This is a sensitive area and one in which little research has been done, but enough is known to make this convenient view untenable. The student's survival in an institution is dependent upon how far he can perceive the institution as providing an experience which is both relevant to his goals and consistent with his personal integrity. Institutions can fall short in these terms due to unrealistic expectations or fantasies on the part of the student; but they can also fall short in reality, in terms of straightforward inefficiency in teaching methods (for example, of courses too difficult, or too easy, or badly structured). Even where a university provides adequate teaching and social facilities, some students may not succeed in utilizing them because the society is too complex, unstructured and confusing. Investigation here is complex but deserves to be carried out on a far wider scale than is now the case. In one interesting study at the Massachusetts Institute of Technology, Snyder[53, 54] demonstrated that students who left certain engineering courses which were specially designed to foster originality were in fact significantly *more* likely to have shown original and creative types of thinking and problem-solving, according to certain tests. This observation must at the very least call into question some of the methods and assumptions of those particular courses. Without specific inquiry, phenomena of this type will seldom be identified. Good teaching demands continual monitoring.

Predisposing Factors in the Student

Evidence about the nature of the problems among students which are associated with wastage is fairly well documented and, apart from discrepancies which probably reflect differences in the institution studied, or in the criteria used, reasonably consistent. Most writers agree that drop-outs include a significantly high proportion of those with personality or emotional problems.[8, 38, 43, 49, 50, 58] Estimates, where given, suggest that in Britain psychiatric illness may account for at least one-third of all wastage, with minor disturbances having some influence in a substantial proportion of the remainder. Clear identification of other relevant background factors is lacking, except for family problems (usually associated with psychiatric and emotional disturbances) such as excessive parental pressures, a bad early relationship with the parents or disruption of the parental marriage. Low social class, with attendant conflicts over motivation, may sometimes be important but the evidence here is conflicting. Lower ability, as measured both by intelligence tests and by academic record, shows some association with wastage, though this is less marked than might be expected.[9] Lucas and his colleagues[29] found that among students dropping out, those who had suffered little or no emotional disturbance scored, on average, somewhat lower than non-wastage controls on a test of high grade intelligence, whereas those with marked emotional disturbance scored nearly as high as controls. This suggests that in the absence of emotional causes of failure relative lack of ability can play some part in dropping out. It also suggests that lack of ability is not in itself a general cause of emotional problems.

Where a university accepts students from a wide ability range, intellectual factors are likely to play a significant part in determining drop-out rates and in determining which student will drop out, whereas in a university creaming off only the most able (and this means most British universities), the student who drops out is more likely to have emotional rather than intellectual difficulties.

THE INTERRUPTERS

The student who, after a period of absence, due either to illness or his own choice, resumes his career at the same or another institution, is likely to share characteristics with the wastage group on the one hand and with the less severely disrupted academic difficulty group, discussed below, on the other hand. Once again the position varies according to which side of the Atlantic you are on, for interruption and resumption of courses tends to be frowned upon in Britain, whereas it seems to be a frequent and more acceptable phenomenon in the United

States. The study of this group of students has been largely confined to America where many authors, while recognizing that the decision to withdraw is often an unreasonable one related to emotional or identity problems, concede that the experience may be a constructive one which can lead to personality growth. How do these interrupters fare on their return?

Powell,[45] in a study of fifty Harvard Interrupters in whom psychiatric factors had operated, presents the only factual evidence I have come across to indicate which type of student is likely to resume successfully if readmitted. His conclusions, though based on a small sample in one institution, seem to be in line with the impressions of many others and are therefore worth quoting, although in need of confirmation and replication. He found that pre-university school achievement, and intelligence as tested at intake, did not predict successful graduation in the interrupter who returned to university, whereas the academic record in the first year at university was significantly predictive. The chances of successful return did not depend upon the category of psychiatric illness. The factors most closely related to success were duration of absence (absence of less than a full year having a bad outcome) and the use made by the student of the interval. Those who had been in steady employment in a structured job did better than those who had worked in an unstructured, interrupted way or who had not followed any employment.

ACADEMIC PROBLEM GROUP

When we come to consider academic difficulty of a less severe level, not leading to withdrawal, firm evidence is again hard to come by. Notification of the student in academic difficulty will occur only when the system ensures that tutors are on the lookout for it and the criteria will vary greatly between different institutions. For this section I am drawing largely on work carried out with the assistance of Martin Lunghi at the University of Sussex.[50] In this work we studied all cases of wastage, interruption and academic difficulty occurring in one year's intake of students. We had the advantage of close liaison with tutorial staff. The university applies a reasonably standard operational criterion of academic difficulty in that students at serious risk of failure, or not meeting course requirements, are all reported to a central committee – the Student Progress Committee. In addition, psychometric testing of all students is carried out at intake and nearly all undergraduates are looked after by the university health service which provides both general medical and psychiatric cover. It is our policy to encourage both direct consultation and referral by tutors of students in academic difficulty.

The operational criteria of academic difficulty and of illness were as follows. A student was classified as in *academic difficulty* where he withdrew for any reason from the university (wastage and interrupters) or where his difficulty was of a degree sufficient to warrant his being reported to the university's Student Progress Committee. Students were classified as *psychiatric patients* when, having been assessed in the university health service, they were deemed to need either hospital admission, or four or more treatment sessions for a psychiatric disorder.

Tests taken by all students at entry to university included a high-grade verbal intelligence measure, the Eysenck Personality Inventory,[16] giving measures of neuroticism (tendency to emotional instability and psychiatric illness) and extraversion (sociability and expressiveness) and the Nufferno Speed Tests.[20] These are tests of reasoning given under two conditions, once without time pressure and once with. Normal subjects perform better under time stress, the improvement being measured as the stress gain.

Findings

There were two main groups of problem students of approximately equal size. The first consisted of those who had presented with psychiatric disturbance. The mean scores of this group on verbal intelligence and on the unstressed Nufferno Test were higher than those of the control group, but not significantly. Their scores on the Nufferno Test under time stress dropped – that is to say there was a negative stress gain. Most of this group took Finals. The second group, the academic difficulty group, two thirds of whom were drop-outs, differed significantly from the control group only in showing a *higher* stress gain on the Nufferno Tests; in each case controls were drawn from the same intake of students and matched for sex and faculty. The mean neuroticism scores of the first group were higher than those of the control group, and for the second group the mean extraversion scores were higher than for the control group; however, in neither case was the difference statistically significant. The findings in respect of the stress gain measure are discussed below.

FAILURES

It is well known that some psychiatric patients do well in university Finals examinations; it is also well known that they are represented disproportionately amongst the failures. More detailed data, however, is sparse. I am therefore basing this section also on my own limited work and it would clearly be unwise to generalize too far from this restricted sample. The intake of students which was the subject of the above investigation was followed through to Finals, and the fate of the two problem groups described above was compared to that of the rest of the intake group as a whole. The great majority of students who actually took Finals did succeed in graduating, but, despite their equivalent or higher intelligence, they tended to have a poorer class of degree than did the intake population as a whole.

As regards scores on psychological tests, over the whole population (for both arts and science students) degree class and extraversion were significantly, negatively, correlated, that is to say extraverts did relatively poorly as compared to introverts. Neuroticism was not associated with degree class. Whether extraversion reduces academic achievement by virtue of some typical effect upon motivation or whether extraverts just spend too much time at parties or playing games is not clear. The students who failed, as opposed to those obtaining low class degrees, were significantly more neurotic and more introverted than was the population as a whole.

CONCLUSION

From the evidence available it looks as if, under British conditions, lack of adequate intelligence does not seem to present a large problem, but there are two main, distinct groups of students in whom persistence, motivation or performance are impaired. In the first group there are the students with psychiatric or emotional problems. Detailed consideration of the way in which work is interfered with in these students is provided subsequently in Chapter 8. At this point one can note that the drop in performance under time stress on the Nufferno Test summarizes what is experienced clinically as true, namely that these students are disorganized by stress and anxiety. In the second group one finds emotionally stable, somewhat extra-verted students who show a propensity to drop out and to under-achieve. In this group, performance on the Nufferno Test under stress is markedly better than under no pressure, which could indicate a usual level of anxiety that is too low for efficient work. What sort of institutional sticks or carrots might be effective in improving the performance of this kind of student is not known.

These two groups of under-achieving students as operationally defined, account for about ten per cent of the university population at Sussex and it is likely that they represent the tip of an even larger iceberg of under-achievement. If we add to this number the drop-outs – seven per cent at Sussex, thirteen per cent on average nationally, we can see that the problem is a serious one.

The formulations and classifications put forward in this chapter are crude in the extreme and anyone with a concern for raising the true productivity of universities, that is to say with improving the quality and quantity of graduates, must be impatient for more detailed and subtle studies. One moral is, however, plain; failing students may differ widely in the cause of their failure, and teachers must have a repertoire of responses for them. To enable tutors to exercise this discrimination, universities must provide a teaching environment in which the appropriate tutorial skills can be developed. A reduction in academic casualty rates can only be achieved by combining a concern for the problem of the individual student with a continuing critical self-examination of the university's performance and practices.

6   Psychiatric Illness in Students
– Psychotic Illness

It is not intended to provide a comprehensive account of all the psychiatric disorders to which the student may be liable, as this would involve writing half a psychiatric textbook, but certain overall features are of importance if the impact of illness upon the student's life is to be understood. It is therefore my intention to summarize some facts about the major types of disorder and their treatment of the outcome of treatment, bearing in mind the sorts of information which may be of use to the teacher or to the student. This present chapter will describe the main forms of psychotic illness and the next chapter will deal with neurosis and personality disorder. The chapter following that will focus upon academic difficulty caused by psychiatric problems, in view of the particular importance of this aspect in the university context.

One or two per cent of students will be affected by a serious, possibly psychotic, illness, during their university career, and this quite usually will be the first manifestation of the illness in the student's lifetime. The commonest of such illnesses are schizophrenia on the one hand and the affective (manic-depressive) psychoses on the other. The actual illnesses of individuals are less clear-cut than systems of classification, and in this age-group particularly a mixed picture is not uncommon, showing some features of schizophrenia and some more typical of manic-depression. A further group of students may experience brief, short-lived episodes marked by psychotic features which seem to represent extreme forms of late adolescent identity crises. An example from this group is presented in the next chapter.

SCHIZOPHRENIA

The causes of schizophrenia are uncertain and are the subject of much debate. Genetic studies suggest that inherited predisposition is one of the necessary conditions for the illness to develop, though the mode of inheritance is uncertain and is not explicable in terms of a simple Mendelian model. Studies of the family environments of schizophrenic patients[36, 37, 42] suggest that these are usually disturbed. Communication between the patient and his parents and more generally within the family is marked by a pervasive ambiguity and confusion. The patient's sense of identity and worth is undermined by the contradictory demands and expectations of the rest of the family and his madness may be seen as a retreat from this situation or as an unsuccessful attempt to make sense of it. The evidence that such distortions of communication in the family precede the illness of the sick member, or that they are causally related to it is not yet satisfactorily established, but enough is known to make it imperative that such factors be considered in any future research. On the other hand, simple biochemical theories attributing the disease to an inborn error of metabolism have been no better validated.

The majority of schizophrenic patients have, prior to their breakdown, been somewhat abnormal, withdrawn people showing difficulty in coping with relationships and sometimes being eccentric or preoccupied with bizarre ideas. The illness itself may be ushered in by an exaggeration of these traits before the symptoms of frank breakdown develop. These symptoms affect mood, thinking and the patient's perception of the self, of the physical environment and of others. Mood is characterized by the absence of intense feeling, or by the demonstration of feeling which is apparently inappropriate to the context (though sometimes explicable if the patient's perception of what is going on can be shared). Thinking is marked by slowness, by a tendency to block, or shift to a different topic and by the illogical development of ideas sometimes described as 'knight's move' thinking. Distortions of perception may include a change in the patient's body image and a loss in the clear differentiation between the self and the world around. Sensations may be interpreted as being due to outside influences or internal events, or thoughts may be experienced as having an effect upon the outside world. Ideas and thoughts may be felt as foreign to the patient and may be attributed to others, usually as having hostile intent. Delusions of this sort may be accompanied by hallucinations, most characteristically of voices.

A student going into a frank schizophrenic breakdown is likely to present a marked alteration in his appearance, behaviour and work and on these counts is likely to be identified as ill by those teaching him. Severely disturbed behaviour will be obvious but equally significant distortions of thinking, especially if expressed in philosophical speculations, may appear to the teacher to represent no more than an extreme variety of commonly encountered late adolescent preoccupations. In such cases the accessibility of a doctor able to give diagnostic advice is a necessary support for the teacher.

In a majority of cases of schizophrenic breakdown hospitalization will be necessary, usually for some months. Treatment will consist primarily of drugs, particularly those developed over the past fifteen to twenty years. These drugs have the affect of diminishing the patient's abnormal experiences and behaviour. Psychotherapy of a schizophrenic patient is very seldom carried out (in Britain, anyway) and is considered positively harmful by many. A schizophrenic's basic defect can be described as ego-weakness, which is a way of saying that those aspects of personality concerned with a mediation between inner drives and experience and the environment are markedly impaired. Because of this, psychotherapists are denied an ally in the patient, who remains at the mercy of his inner forces and is confused by the blurring of inner and outer reality. The group setting within which the schizophrenic patient is cared for is, however, of great importance. Much of the severe deterioration once considered typical of chronic schizophrenia is now known to be the effect of the insensitive, restrictive and impoverished environments which were offered in many mental hospitals. In a more positive sense, some believe that to allow a schizophrenic some expression of his thoughts and impulses within a supportive group setting may be therapeutic.

With modern treatment the majority of schizophrenics will be able to leave hospital after a few months. The readmission rate is high but nearly two out of three patients can hope to recover enough to stay outside hospital permanently. In the case of schizophrenic students, early return to work and to the stresses of university life is definitely a mistake, but about half may eventually be able to resume their studies.

A Case of Schizophrenia

William first presented to the clinic in his second year, complaining of depression and difficulty in thinking. He had had a serious depression three years previously and had at that time made a suicidal bid. In recent months he had decided to 'adopt a new identity', but he still felt that his potential was badly blocked and still felt unable to fully understand other people. In his first interview he spoke of his parents with anger and described how early on at the university he had become attached to and dependent on one of his tutors. Further assessment in this case gave evidence of a deep confusion about sexual identity, but he had difficulty in coping with interviews and broke off contact. Over the ensuing weeks his thoughts became increasingly muddled. He began to invent new words, the meaning of which he could not clearly define. He reappeared and was referred for Rorschach testing (the test in which the patients' associations to a standard set of inkblots are interpreted). His responses on this test were of a markedly psychotic nature and gave confirmatory evidence of his deep confusion about his body image and sexuality.

A short time after this he made a suicidal threat and was admitted to hospital under certificate. In hospital he was treated with tranquillizers and electro-convulsive therapy. Interviews with his parents at this stage revealed them as apparently incapable of accepting or acknowledging the serious nature of William's illness. Subsequently they colluded with him in attributing all his symptoms to the treatment he had received and eventually they took him from hospital against advice, though they later requested urgently that he should be re-admitted.

Contact with his tutors was made after admission to hospital. (He had refused permission for such contact before.) His tutorial reports showed that his confusion and thought disorder had been manifest in obscure, bizarre, often incomprehensible essays for several months before his clinical presentation. Thus he wrote essays which 'at their best are laboured and unoriginal, sometimes quite dislocated and incoherent'; he was 'painfully shy' and he had a 'strangely inconsequential grasshopper mind, moving in one paragraph from real critical insight to complete stupidity.'

One year after his admission to hospital and six months after his discharge from in-patient care, William applied for re-admission to the university with his parents' support. A report from the psychiatrist in charge of the case revealed definite improvement, but noted a persistence of some symptoms despite medication. At an interview at that time he displayed several odd mannerisms, he frequently lost his train of thought and he showed little feeling or responsiveness. On the basis of this a further delay before readmission was advised.

A year later, still under medication, he returned to the university and despite some persistent peculiarities in his behaviour he proved able to function at an adequate level and went on to complete his course.

AFFECTIVE PSYCHOSES
(*Manic-Depression*)

These illnesses are characterized by changes – often cyclic – in affect – that is to say in mood and feeling. Genetic studies suggest that inheritance plays a significant part in the production of affective psychoses as with schizophrenia; but both the precise limits of this entity and its mode of transmission remain ill-defined. The illness appears to be the result of a disturbance in the brain centres responsible for the regulation and rhythmic changes of a large number of physiological functions and for the regulation of mood and can be seen as an exaggeration of the normal ups and downs of mood. Individual attacks of depression or of hypomanic or manic behaviour (marked by over-excitable, restless, distractable behaviour) may be provoked by physical events such as childbirth, surgical operations or virus infections, or by extreme psychological stresses such as bereavement, but many cases seem to arise spontaneously, sometimes showing a strong cyclical tendency with episodes recurring at intervals of days, weeks, months, or years. In those prone to repeated attacks there is a tendency for the frequency of attacks to increase with age. Subjects may have only manic or only depressive attacks, but many experience both, and swings from one state to the other are common.

Affective psychoses tend to occur in those of normal or robust personality. These patients do not give a history of preceding withdrawal or eccentricity, such as is found in the case of schizophrenia. The 'up' phase is marked by an increased energy and cheerfulness, which, for a time, may be accompanied by a greater efficiency and output. In the student this may be reflected in high achievement, though more often the energy is diverted to projects outside the course. In a mild attack the cheerfulness can be engaging and the quick thinking, often jumping across conventional boundaries, can be stimulating. But the insistent, relentless pressure of talk and the illogicalities and tangents pursued become wearing to the listener, and one soon observes that the patient's behaviour is becoming unrealistic and uncharacteristic. In students this phase may be marked by preoccupations with ultimate truths and insights, and sometimes after recovery these episodes are looked back upon as having been constructive. In the acute manic state, insomnia and incessant motor activity may make hospitalization urgent, and in milder cases the patient may need admission as a defence against potentially damaging decisions and behaviour, for example, rash expenditure, or promiscuity.

The depressive phase of the manic-depressive illness may be less easily identified, and there is still some controversy among doctors as to the relationship between the depression due to affective psychosis (endogenous depression) and the depression resulting from psychological stresses (reactive depression). Some argue for a unitary view of depression whereas others believe that two distinct entities exist. Most writers would agree that one can distinguish, within the group of depressed patients, some in whom the depression is profound, associated with self-reproach and guilt, and with disturbances of sleep rhythm, appetite, bowel function and sexual interest. Attacks may recur at intervals without any apparent cause. These patients may themselves feel that the depression happened to them like an illness or like a punishment, rather than viewing it as the result of problems in their life. At the other extreme, one finds depressed patients who, while sharing some of the same symptoms, are clearly experiencing losses or difficulties or restrictions in their life of a degree sufficient to make their change in mood explicable. In between these two extremes of patients there are many exhibiting both reactive features and symptoms suggesting endogenous factors. It is by no means easy to disentangle the operation of these two factors. For example, a mild endogenous depression may blunt the patient's capacity to respond to his life situation or to cope with problems which are in fact long-standing and which were previously contained adequately. Such a patient may end up in a stressful situation which is the result rather than the cause of his trouble.

The patient with a mild endogenous depression may present without any complaint of sadness, though he may well have observed an uncharacteristic flatness and lack of responsiveness. Sleep disturbance is common, particularly marked by a proneness to wake early, which is followed by a prolonged period of inertia in the early part of the day. Loss of appetite, digestive upsets and a lack of sexual interest may all be present to some extent. The student in this state may continue to turn in some work, though both quantity and quality are likely to be impaired, and the nine o'clock lecture presents a particular problem (though this is true of many who are not suffering from this condition!). The more severely depressed patient will have the same symptoms with an addition of deep melancholy. He views the future as hopeless and is filled with guilt and self-reproach. The failing student who offers himself for expulsion because of his poor work may, at times, fall into this category.

In a proportion of patients, both hypomanic and depressive phases may be seen, the former often being followed by the latter. To an extent the hypomanic state may be seen as an attempt to defend against depression – a desperate effort to see all things as possible and no obstacle too high to overcome, in contrast to depression where the capacity of the self to cope with even ordinary demands is doubted.

As regards treatment, the patient who is suffering from an affective psychosis can be helped with drugs or he may, in severe cases, need electro-convulsive therapy. Drugs of the tranquillizing group may damp down the hypomanic attack, while anti-depressants often relieve the depressive state. Any depressed patient in whom there is clear evidence of a physiological component in the depression should be given drug therapy; even though such a patient presents with psychological problems these may often prove to be soluble without psychotherapeutic help, or to be irrelevant, once the physiological depression has been controlled. In cases where it is not clear whether endogenous factors operate or not, drug therapy may still be given a trial provided adequate psychiatric investigation is carried out. Psychotherapy may in fact be facilitated by drug treatment in such cases. With a patient who becomes depressed in the course of psychotherapy the position is somewhat different. Depression here may represent the acknowledgement and working through of earlier losses and difficulties, and the experience of this sadness in the context of a psychotherapeutic relationship can be a constructive one.

The great majority of students who develop either hypomanic or depressive illnesses will recover and be able to complete their course, but many will need additional time or periods of absence. This group of patients, most of whom can be expected to proceed to productive careers (even though they may experience subsequent episodes of illness) emphasizes once more the need for adequate medical screening of all failing students.

A Case of Affective Psychosis – Hypomanic Attack

Elizabeth was seen during her first term at the urgent request of the Senior Proctor, whose room she had invaded and refused to leave. She was trying to persuade him to abolish his office because it would no longer be necessary now that she had discovered the power of love. This power would also enable her, it appeared, to live on water only and would guarantee that summer would never end. She was unwilling to accept medication and hospitalization did not seem immediately necessary, so she was seen daily for some days and subsequently at longer intervals. During this period she surprised her tutors, on the rare occasions on which she attended tutorials, with the exuberance of her thinking, and she worried her landlady by the irregular hours she kept and her frequent nocturnal excursions. To her fellow students she seemed to have provided a source of cheerful support. This girl's omnipotent ideas and her denial of all things evil in the world, diminished after the first few days and some two months later she had reached a mildly depressed mood and was much preoccupied with her own inadequacy and insignificance. It appeared that during the year before coming to university she had been rather unhappy, and there were a number of family problems which she had been coping with, exacerbated by the fact that her mother had recently been hospitalized with a depressive illness, which had been treated with electro-convulsive therapy. After the hypomanic attack had subsided, this patient was given supportive psychotherapy over the next year. Over this period, she showed no further sign of psychotic disturbance beyond the mild depression and functioned normally, socially and academically, though her responses to ideas and to people continued, to some extent, to show a tendency towards polarization into extreme, either – or, concepts. She graduated with an upper second degree.

This case is a typical short-lived mild hypomanic illness, followed by a mild depressive illness, occurring in a girl with a family history of affective psychosis; in this case the illness settled without medication.

A Case of Affective Psychosis – Mild Depression with Endogenous Features

Douglas consulted five weeks before his first-year preliminary examinations. He complained of a long-standing lack of energy, which led to his often falling asleep during the afternoon. His sleep at night was disturbed and on waking he felt exhausted and took two or three hours to come round. He did not complain of being depressed, though he said he was somewhat anxious about the examination, but he did report that whereas previously he had been a cheerful and sociable character, he was now 'a shocking introvert'. He had, in the past year, unexpectedly failed his 'A' levels and had to repeat the year. He described good family relationships, and he was engaged, but his fiancée was at the time spending a year in the United States, and he was missing her.

He was treated with an anti-depressant drug and over the next three weeks he began to sleep well, woke up feeling refreshed and no longer needed his afternoon sleep, and he stopped worrying unnecessarily about the exam, for which he was in fact now working effectively.

The physiological disturbance and the response to anti-depressants suggests this was a mild endogenous depression. The anxiety not to repeat his examination failure may have been a provoking factor, but with the relief of the depression he was able to function perfectly well.

SCHIZO-AFFECTIVE DISORDERS

Sub-divisions of psychosis in the student age group are less definite than in older age groups and a fairly large proportion of cases will present with both schizophrenic and manic-depressive features. Schizophrenic symptoms are often marked but there is usually less evidence of abnormal personality in the past. The family history may contain examples of depressive illness (possibly also of schizophrenia). The outlook for recovery for these cases is better than it is in the case of schizophrenia, however florid the initial illness. If subsequent attacks of illness occur they are likely to show increasingly depressive rather than schizophrenic symptomatology.

A Case of Schizo-Affective Breakdown with a Depressive Second Attack

Elaine presented early in her second year, saying she was troubled with thoughts and with intense prolonged images, mostly of a sexual nature. These thoughts and images, she felt, had no connection with her proper thoughts. In recent weeks she had become increasingly cut-off from other people; she had never had any close friends or any girl-friends. She now felt so guilty about the nature of her thoughts that she preferred to avoid close contact with anybody. She was seen again two days later, having been treated with a tranquillizer; she now said she was confused and her thoughts were disconnected, she had lost her memory for people's names and she described fantasies of insects boring at her skull. In speaking at this time, she was hesitant, often lost the train of thought and seemed preoccupied. Tutors' reports recorded 'sparks of originality from her laborious flint' and 'a great deal of latent ability' right up to the breakdown.

Her parents were summoned and arrangements were made for treatment near her home. In the intervening period she became very anxious that the drugs she had been treated with might have harmed her and she telephoned the police on this account. There was no previous history of any serious disharmony in the immediate family, but a grandparent and an aunt had both had in-patient psychiatric treatment; the diagnosis of the conditions from which they had suffered was not known.

She was treated with in-patient care, drugs and electro-convulsive therapy in a hospital near her home and subsequently had psychotherapy from the consultant in charge of her case, who gave the diagnosis of schizo-affective disorder. After a year's absence from the university, she was able to return and resume her work adequately, though not quite up to the high standard of her first year, but it was noticeable that her speech and gait were still less fluent than previously; she remained on drug treatment. During her second year back at the university her work began to deteriorate, she became depressed and began to reproach herself for her failure to do better, and also began to neglect her appearance. On this occasion, a small number of treatments with electro-convulsive therapy produced a rapid return to a more normal state and she was able to continue to work satisfactorily and to obtain a second class degree. In this case the initial illness presented a number of features suggestive of schizophrenia, but the second attack was more clearly depressive in nature.

HELPING THE PSYCHOTIC PATIENT

In concluding this chapter on the psychoses it is important to emphasize that, except for mild depressions, they are relatively rare. Most people who are worried about going mad have no need to do so. I would remind the anxious reader who may have used the above descriptions as a check list for his own feelings, that diagnosis in this field is not simply based upon the identification of one or two characteristic symptoms.

A psychotic illness is always a serious matter, even though modern treatment has greatly improved this outlook, especially in the case of the affective psychoses. Early treatment is important if tragedies are to be avoided, and dissatisfaction with the very real deficiencies of the mental hospital services should not be used to justify delay. Dissatisfaction with staffing and facilities is general; more recently, writers such as Laing,[33, 34, 36] have emphasized social and philosophical deficiencies also, castigating the psychiatric profession for its failure to recognize or attempt to understand the communications of the psychotic patient. This important criticism has lost some of its force by being taken to an extreme position,[35] in which the psychotic is elevated to a position of particular virtue in our mad society, and in which conventional treatments are dismissed as society's attempts to suppress the individual into blind conformity. The psychiatrist has become, in the view of some underground writers, the last in a line of social oppressors. This is an absurdly exaggerated view. The psychotic patient inhabits a world where his perceptions are dislocated and his discriminations blurred, in which other people are out of reach or menacing; whatever the cause of his condition he is suffering from a complex impairment of function and the concept of illness is an appropriate one with which to consider his problems. Any therapy which can diminish this impairment and reduce his suffering should be used.

Psychiatric Illness in Students—Neurosis and Personality Problems

Personality problems and neurotic illness represent by far the most common psychiatric disorders at all ages and students, as has been indicated earlier, are no exception. A description of personality represents a generalized statement about a person's mode of life, summarizing the ways in which he tends to go about his affairs and relate to others. A neurotic illness is marked by symptoms (mood change, physical discomfort, etc.) and by difficulties in coping with other people. In the student age group, where personality formation is not yet complete, the distinction between illness and personality deviation is often difficult to make.

SOURCES OF VARIATION IN PERSONALITY

An individual's personality is always the result of the combined effects of his inheritance and his life experience. Observations of children from birth onwards have shown how certain attributes are present from the earliest days, for example, the level of activity, the wish to explore, distractability, and the ability to cope with strange situations seem consistent characteristics. Investigations of the personalities of identical twins have shown a high degree of similarity even when the children have been reared apart. However, inborn attributes do not act on their own; from the earliest days they will influence the child's behaviour towards his parents and so evoke different responses. Parents, in any case, will vary a great deal in the way in which they bring up their children and this too can have an effect, as Burton,[5] having acknowledged the importance of inheritance, wrote in 1621:

> Parents and such as have the tuition and oversight of children, offend many times in that they are too sterne, always threatning, chiding, brawling, whipping or striking; by meanes of which their poore children are so disheartened and cowed that they never after have any courage or a merry houre in their lives or take pleasure in anything. ... Others againe in that other extreame doe as much harme. Too much indulgence causeth the like, many fond mothers especially, dote so much upon their children like Aesop's ape 'til in the end they crush them to death.

THE CLASSIFICATION OF PERSONALITY

Descriptions of normal personality in terms of a limited number of dimensions are of respectable antiquity; little more than its factor analytic gloss distinguishes Eysenck's two-dimensional description in terms of stable versus neurotic, and introverted versus extraverted, from ancient theories describing people's temperaments according to their share of the four humours, blood, phlegm, choler and black bile. Classifications of this sort are of use in comparing populations but in studying individuals more complex theories or models are needed. Such theories tend to pay more attention to the way in which the individual interacts with others, and to be less concerned with the elaboration of descriptions of traits. A criticism of such descriptions is that they often fail to provide a basis for classification or comparison.

Extreme variations in personality, in which behaviour is abnormal enough to lead to referral to psychiatrists or to trouble with the law, are classified descriptively. The main categories of abnormal personality are: *schizoid personality* characterized by the avoidance of close contact with others, *paranoid personality* characterized by suspiciousness, *cyclothymic personality* characterized by variations in mood and energy level, *psychopathy* – either characterized by inadequacy or by anti-social tendencies, and *sexual deviancy*. Of these abnormal personality types the schizoid, cyclothymic and sexual deviant may be found in a student population. Mild forms of the others do occur but severe examples are uncommon, presumably due to the prolonged process of educational selection.

NEUROSIS – WHAT ARE THE CAUSES?

The causes of neurotic illness are complex and varied. In many ways the neurotic is only differentiated from the normal in degree rather than in kind. This is sometimes expressed by saying that everybody is neurotic in some way, but such a statement robs the term of value, so some criterion of abnormality must be applied. This criterion may be to do with symptoms, or it may be defined in terms of the quality of the individual's life and relationships. A strictly medical approach will favour the former type, whereas the psychodynamic approach will favour the latter. In psychodynamic terms, a neurotic is someone whose capacity to develop as a person in relation to others and to pursue his aims in life is impaired due to emotional causes.

Genetic factors probably play an important part in determining the type of neurotic symptoms developed by a given individual, but whether or not neurosis develops is much more a question of the individual's early experience of others, particularly in the family setting. While clear prospective studies linking specific child-rearing practices or family patterns to specific patterns of subsequent neurotic disorder are lacking, there is a large volume of highly suggestive research[55] indicating that emotional disturbance of some sort in the childhood home plays a critical role in the genesis of neurosis. The relation of such disturbance to adult neurosis is obviously a complex one. Basically, the neurotic is someone who continues to operate in relation to others in terms derived from his early experience. According to the account given in Chapter 3 of Erikson's theories, one sees how the neurotic, when faced with another person, structures the relationship in terms dictated by his childhood, according to his degree of basic trust or distrust, according to how far he feels forced to be compliant or defiant, and according to how far he is secure in his sex role and realistic in his expectations of the behaviour and role of others. The neurotic maintains a primitive structure or model of relation-ships by selecting the type of relationship he engages in and by effectively perceiving only those aspects of others which accord with his basic assumptions and fantasies. He has 'learned not to learn', at least as regards personal relations.

In adolescence, neurotic illness often takes the form of an identity crisis – a state in which the individual's sense of who he is or where he is going is lost. The adolescent in this state may attempt to find himself by a return to childhood dependence or by a bewildering succession of group affiliations or personal attachments.

CLINICAL PRESENTATION AND CLASSIFICATION
OF THE NEUROSES

The neurotic may present, therefore, in a variety of ways, according to his genetic make-up, the nature of his conflicts and the roles of the other people with whom his is particularly in-volved. If his life situation is favourable, he may be able to maintain a reasonable balance, but a change – in his job, or in an important relationship – can upset this balance and lead to ' decompensation'. In such phases of decompensation he may be obviously ill in the sense of displaying physical and psycho-logical symptoms. But at other times he may appear to be behaving stupidly, irrationally, or bloody-mindedly or he may, at least in a more or less structured relationship, appear to be entirely normal. He may at times be able to preserve himself from symptoms by evading closeness to others, or he may cope with relationships by forcing the other to carry his confusion, or by provoking the other into playing the one-dimensional part demanded by his fantasy system.

To understand what the neurotic's illness means a doctor will need to build up a view of the patient's history, relationships and mode of construing himself and others. This latter under-standing will involve going beneath the surface appearances and unravelling fantasies and assumptions of which the patient himself may be unaware. Parallel with this evaluation the psychological mechanisms and symptoms which the patient displays will be noted, for these determine the strategy and, to some extent, predict the outcome of therapy.

Descriptive classifications of neurotic disorders differ considerably in different countries and between different schools of thought. Even among those sharing a particular system or outlook, the categorization of a given patient may show rather low agreement between different observers. Basically all classifications of this sort depend upon noting the presence or absence of the following features:

Neurotic Anxiety

An anxiety reaction represents serious anxiety provoked by a specific event or situation. An anxiety state represents a more pervasive and less specifically provoked mood disturbance.

Depression

The classification of neurotic depression parallels that of neurotic anxiety.

Phobic Reactions

Phobias, namely irrational fears of specific situations or objects, may occur as one aspect of an anxiety state, in which case they are most commonly fears of either closed or open spaces. Phobias may, however, be more narrowly specific, to particular animals or objects, although such phobias seldom occur without some other evidence of psychological disturbance. The restricted type of phobia is often best treated with methods based upon learning theory.

Obsessive Compulsive Reactions

An obsessive compulsive neurosis is a form of neurosis which is likely to be persistent, disabling and resistant to treatment. The patient suffers from an irresistible urge to repeat certain actions or phrases, or finds his thoughts are compelled along

certain repetitive tracks. Attempts to resist the actions or
thoughts lead to a rise in anxiety and cannot be persisted with.
Minor obsessional symptoms are common in the course of many
neurotic illnesses in which the individual becomes particularly
tidy or rearranges his belongings or develops rituals of various
sorts; these minor forms of obsessionality can often be seen as
an attempt to preserve some kind of constancy in a shifting
world. In more severe forms, the obsessional thoughts and
rituals can dominate the patient's life.

Hysteria

Hysterical symptoms are characterized by a loss of function of
some sort, affecting sensation, speech, vision, movement, or
mimicking epilepsy or a host of other organic diseases. It is as
if the patient invents his own disease according to his idea of
some condition, or according to the need he has of some dis-
ability to gain an end or avoid a situation. In the fashionable
hey-day of hysteria seventy years ago, this condition provided
a good living for neurologists and for charlatans. Hysterical
symptoms of a gross kind are no longer fashionable or common
in Western countries, an observation which throws an interesting light on the effect of culture upon psychiatric symptomatology.

Neurosis with Somatic Symptoms

Neurotic anxiety or neurotic depression are often accompanied
by somatic symptoms and, at times, may be linked with frank
psychosomatic disorders, like peptic ulcers and asthma, in
which psychological factors can play an important part.

Hypochondriasis

In some chronic neurotics the concern with bodily discomforts
and anxiety about bodily functions may be extreme; these cases
are labelled hypochondriasis.

In the case histories at the end of this chapter, examples will be given of some of these types of neurotic disorder; psychodynamic formulations will also be provided in these accounts.

TREATMENT OF NEUROSIS

Treatment of most neurotic patients, especially in the student age-group, is ideally psycho-therapeutic. Drugs may temporarily relieve symptoms and this, at times, can be of value in preventing the development of secondary problems and under many circumstances may be the only practicable response. But fundamentally, the resolution of a neurosis demands the modification of the individual's view of himself and others. This involves a relationship with the therapist or with a therapeutic group in which the restrictions and distortions of his perceptions can be exposed and not colluded with. At the same time the experience of a firm, supportive relationship in therapy can resolve the distrusts, defiances or confusions which underlie these distortions. Of course many neurotics, especially adolescent neurotics, may experience relationships in a non-clinical setting to facilitate these changes for them. Often, however, the pattern of difficulty and failure is repeated over and over again, or projects of critical importance to the individual's development are blocked by the neurosis; the student in serious work difficulty provides one such example. In these cases therapeutic intervention may be essential to assist the individual towards a more workable and rewarding existence. The student age-group represents a particularly fertile time for such intervention because personality structure is still fluid and relationships are less fixed and immutable than is the case at any other age.

THE COURSE OF NEUROSIS

The outcome of neurosis in terms of the student's viability in the university has been discussed in earlier chapters. The critical factors in the individual which determine the outlook are, firstly, the degree of deprivation or privation experienced in childhood and how early in life it was experienced (severe and early problems generally presenting a much larger therapeutic problem) and, secondly, the capacity of the patient to use the experience of treatment. This capacity is a function of what is called ego-strength, a quality which therapists are better at recognizing than defining. Many neurotics, whether treated or not, will continue throughout their lives to demonstrate to some degree neurotic patterns of behaviour, or will have to restrict their lives or rely on the support of others if they are to preserve a reasonable equilibrium. Treatment can at least aim to diminish these restrictions, and can help the neurotic to structure his relationships in ways which are more rewarding and less damaging to himself and others. Satisfactory demonstrations of the efficiency of psychotherapeutic interventions are still few and far between, though less few and far between than the most vocal critics of psychotherapy would like to suggest.[59]

In many cases the aims of treatment have to be relatively modest. Treatment itself is often a disturbing experience and may be best postponed in the student approaching Finals. In cases with fundamental problems, the doctor must often be content to do no more than tide the patient over the episode of decompensation without trying to change the underlying personality or modes relating to others.

NEUROSIS IN STUDENTS

This chapter continues with five case histories (considerably modified in detail to preserve anonymity) of student psychiatric patients chosen to illustrate the themes outlined above. The main aim is to emphasize those aspects which are likely to be most relevant to the student and the teacher. Enough is said, I hope, to give some idea of the family background factors preceding the neurosis and of the impact of the illness on the student's life at university. While the patients described below have a variety of problems, all were suffering from crises of identity in some way. This is to be expected in an age-group engaged in the psychological task of discovering, preserving or confirming their own adult identity in a situation of transition and change.

Case History

Diagnosis: Depressive Reaction; Immature Personality – Sarah presented at the beginning of her second year soon after having had an illegal abortion. This pregnancy was the result of a brief affair with an exploitive, sadistic man. She was unhappy but not remorseful, for she felt that the experience of the pregnancy had stirred feelings in her which she had never before acknowledged. Initially, she did not ask for treatment, but she returned after a few weeks and thereafter received psychotherapy for the next two years. During the first part of this period she continued to behave self-destructively in a number of ways, in particular she was promiscuous and tended to choose partners to whom she was indifferent; she often drank to excess and she indulged in compulsive shop-lifting, the latter symptom having started only after the abortion. Throughout this time, however, she did well in her academic work. As regards her background she was an only child and her father had deserted the mother when the patient was seven years old and had not been heard of since. The mother was a depressed, resentful woman relying upon Sarah for support, and, it seems, insisting that only she was entitled to have feelings. The father's photograph and other relics were kept in the house as a conspicuous reminder of the mother's loss, making him both a hated and an idealized object. Sarah seemed to have coped by learning to relate to others at a superficial level only, until the pregnancy stirred up deeper feelings which she could not understand. Once these feelings were acknowledged, she was unwilling to re-suppress them, however painful. In therapy, she was at first cautious and unwilling to be committed and she did, early on, fail appointments on more than one occasion. She then became more open and more dependent and worked through, especially after vacation absences, her feelings about the ways in which men inevitably left one and let one down. At this time she was, in effect, splitting men into two categories – the dependable ideal father, represented by the therapist, and the exciting, sexual and destructive type, represented by her successive lovers. Beneath this split lay her own sense of her mother's destructiveness and of her mother's rejection and prohibition of her feelings, especially her sexual or angry feelings. Within the continuing therapeutic relationship she began to be able to express some of these forbidden feelings towards the therapist and became in herself more integrated and less detached. After a time, she formed a serious relationship with a fellow student in which she said 'each could forgive what the other could not give'. Her relationship with her mother began to improve. After graduation, she married this fellow student.

This girl was unable to accept her own sexuality except in a destructive context. Her mother had presented to her an idealized fantasy of a father who had also abandoned her, and her mother herself was a model of a woman who was bitter and restricted, and who disallowed the expression of any strong emotion; later, Sarah was able to see her more positive qualities also. The pregnancy exposed to the patient her own capacity to feel and therapy helped her to explore the sources of her self-destructive tendencies and, to some extent, to heal the division within herself. It speaks well for human resilience that all this was achieved simultaneously with an upper second degree!

Case History

Diagnosis – Acute Identity Crisis with Some Psychotic Features – Gilbert, a first-year chemistry student, behaved oddly and was badly behind in his work through most of his first term. A few days after returning for his second term, he disappeared and was finally traced twelve days later to a hotel in North Wales where he had spent his time working on a three-act play in blank verse. He was brought back to the university by his parents and was persuaded to defer his decision about leaving university, and, with some reluctance, he agreed to attend the Health Centre, where he was seen, in all, on seven occasions. At these interviews he was incoherent and laughed defensively or mockingly much of the time. When offered a single suggestion or interpretation, he would accept it with an exaggerated deference. When offered a choice of interpretations he would mime at picking an answer out of a hat, before replying with one of them. He said that inside all was clear to him, but his only concern for the time being was to complete the play he was writing – considerations of health or illness were meaningless. In any case, although he felt that life was a tragic farce, he thought himself to be immortal. The journey away from the university had been a search for necessary privacy in which to come to terms with himself. At this fourth visit, he brought a copy of his play; it was, in a confused way, concerned with the themes of pity, the falseness of most lives (which should be recognized but could not be changed) and with the need to acknowledge what could not be understood.

On the face of it, many features of this case suggested a schizophrenic illness, but against this diagnosis was a sense that many of his ideas were presented primarily to confuse or mock and did not represent delusions. Beneath the surface one glimpsed and at times contacted a warm person. It therefore seemed that this episode represented a severe identity crisis rather than a schizophrenic illness. Coming to university and faced with doing chemistry at a time when his real concern was with art and philosophy, seemed to have served as the trigger to this state. What scanty evidence he provided about his previous history included a rebellious episode at boarding school and an apparently compliant relationship with apparently benign parents. The conflicts seemed to be between the ascribed identity, in this case that of a student of chemistry, and his own sense of his own nature. After attending for a month he refused to come any more, breaking treatment off with an engaging mixture of gratitude and contempt. Under the threat of expulsion from the university, he settled down and worked reasonably well for the remainder of the term. At the end of that time he withdrew from the university and later graduated elsewhere with a third class degree in English Literature; there had been no further episodes of psychiatric instability.

Case History

Diagnosis – Anxiety State; Conflict over Masculinity – Paul consulted initially because of anxiety about his physical development, and specifically because he feared that his genitalia were not normally formed. He had had a moderately late puberty and had received hormone therapy from a previous doctor, although there was no real evidence of endocrine abnormality. He greeted the suggestion that his worries were expressions of psychological factors rather than of physical abnormality with irritation and contempt, but he consented to return for an interview after he had been physically examined and assessed. His estimates of his height and weight were both exaggerated (neither, in fact, was markedly below average) and he spoke in glowing terms of his academic ability and of his success as a prefect at school. Beneath his bluster and his fears of inadequacy, he was a pleasant individual and was soon able to make a useful relationship in psychotherapy, which continued weekly for two terms. He had a younger sister of whom he was fond; he described his father as a disappointed, pathetic man who failed in his job and as a parent, but later on he recalled a good relationship in early childhood. He saw his mother as a strong, possessive person, who, disappointed in her husband, had demanded both compliance and support from the patient. Potency for this student seemed to represent the danger of exposure to damage by women and to involve him also in the humiliation and surpassing of his defeated, but still loved, father. In therapy he had at first challenged my authority, but later he expressed both lack of trust in my concern (an inadequate father) and fear of my power (a potent rival). During his time in treatment he had exhibited arrogant, rude behaviour to one of his tutors and also to the landlord of the house in which he was lodged. During this period, however, he redefined his family role without causing too much upset and he moved into a new social circle in the university, having previously established himself as a compliant clown in the first group he belonged to. After treatment he remained in contact and reported increasingly successful social and heterosexual relationships.

Case History

Diagnosis – Identity Crisis – Depression, Hysteria – Ann arrived at the Health Centre within the first week of being at university, saying she had fainted in the street. She had had 'faints' for the past three years which had been investigated and she had been told that nothing was wrong. She knew they were nervous and went on to talk about her violent, alcoholic father, about her mother – 'a long-suffering nag', and about her drug-peddling brother. She herself was promiscuous, avoiding any persistent relationship. She was seen twice in the following week complaining of having frightening feelings of detachment and unreality; ten days later she swallowed fifty aspirins and had to be admitted to hospital. Thereafter for the rest of her first term and the first part of her second term she was seen in regular weekly psychotherapy. She was at times engaging and expressive but was more often bored, critical or blank. She missed some appointments and often expressed both doubts as to the use of treatment and as to her right to have it. She was similarly largely uncommitted to her tutors, for whom she produced one or two pieces of work which were described as excellent, but often she missed tutorials or sat through them in a glazed, uninvolved way. At her last interview she complained of being overcome with 'waves of emptiness'. She was angry that the treatment had exposed her problems without resolving them. Treatment was discontinued because she decided to withdraw from the university. Later, in a letter, she described how she had spent an aimless year after leaving university before settling into a job. She continued to have transient and largely meaningless relationships, but said that she seldom now felt panic or despair. Life was only tolerable 'if she avoided the painful search for depth or validity.'

This girl, clearly very vulnerable and disturbed before coming to university, could not respond to the new role demanded of her, and developed somatic symptoms, hysterical symptoms, depersonalization and depression; her sexual identity was uncertainly established. In her adolescence she had been assigned a stabilizing role in a disturbed family and one problem about coming to university was that she could no longer play this role and had both her anxiety at leaving the family and her hostility towards them to deal with. More generally in her life she had learnt to avoid the pain, confusion and demands of close relationships by remaining uninvolved. Her evasion of closeness was reflected in her personal life, in her work as a student and in her behaviour as a patient.

Case History

Diagnosis – Depression and Obsessional Symptoms – Walter's depression and slowness prompted his tutor to refer him to the Health Service at the start of his second term. At interview he appeared inexpressive in his movements and voice and gave an account of himself in a slow, relentlessly detailed, inexpressive way. His problem was summarized by his statement that 'the more I get on here, the further I am from there.' 'There' was home – a small industrial town in Durham where he was the eldest of six children. His father was a semi-skilled worker in the town, one of a family who had for generations worked in the coalfields and who preserved a strong family unity. Neither parent had ever been out of the home county for the past twenty-two years, and none of the family had been as far as London. They were proud of Walter, and in no way resented his success. He, however, could not get used to his good fortune. Some of his fellow students were already car owners, while his father had never yet owned a car, and he himself could go to concerts, cinemas or meetings at will. Even his modest social success in being made secretary to a scientific society seemed to fill him with guilt. He had become increasingly withdrawn socially, was working ineffectively and spent hours every day tidying up his room, arranging his books in various ways, according to their size or colour.

In view of the possibility of an endogenous, depressive element he was given an anti-depressant and was seen regularly for supportive psychotherapy. At these sessions his current feelings and events were discussed, in particular the problem of the split between his home and his student life. After some weeks he experienced a phase during which he was, at times, mildly euphoric and light-headed, and at other times preoccupied with anxious, compulsive ruminations about his family. Following this phase he began to explore his feelings about his transition with greater spontaneity. In the subsequent term he reported that he felt that things were now in proportion and he was coping well with his life.

WHO NEEDS PSYCHOTHERAPY?

How can the potential patient, or his friends, decide whether medical help is indicated for emotional problems? Fears of being seen as weak, and fantasies of psychotherapy as representing impermissible self-indulgence may dissuade some in real need. Neurosis itself, with its tendency to lead to the blocking-off of those aspects of reality which are unacceptable, can inhibit the acknowledgement of personal problems. Neurosis, in the form of symptoms or marked mood change, may only be manifest when the defences against recognition are broken down by the pressure of new demands or the loss of a supportive environment or relationship. The individual whose anxiety or depression is excessive or prolonged in the face of the ordinary problems and crises of life; the individual who repeatedly encounters failure in close relationships as a result of over-possessiveness, destructiveness or some other distorting pattern; and the individual whose projects and intentions are blocked by his own self-defeating actions or attitudes; each of these is likely to be operating within a neurotic framework of some sort. He should feel free to seek medical advice, or should, at times, be persuaded to do so by his friends.

When such an individual consults, the doctor will still have to make a decision as to whether psychotherapy, support and drug therapy, or no treatment are indicated. Some people are too disturbed to be accessible to psychotherapy, and in others – such as the student approaching Finals – it may be tactically wiser to postpone it until after graduation. In these, support and appropriate drugs may help tide over the difficult period. Others, though quite acutely disturbed, may not need treatment to recover. In this age-group quite sound personality structures can be strained and can temporarily lose integration, but, given good basic strength, recovery can occur with time and the experience of ordinary relationships. In these cases the doctor can be content to hold a watching brief, perhaps giving support or one or two interpretative sessions as a catalyst to the normal developmental processes which are at work.

Between those too ill to benefit and those too well to need psychotherapy are the individuals whose growth and capacities are blocked due to non-adaptive attitudes, perceptions and emotions which have their roots in unresolved childhood conflicts. Psychotherapy offers this group the chance of recapitulating and resolving their problems in terms of their relationship with the therapist or with the therapeutic group. It is hard to convey how this process works; it is often prolonged and often painful, but for some it can be a deeply constructive experience.

8 How does Psychiatric Disturbance Interfere with Academic Work?

We have seen in Chapter 4 that emotional and psychiatric difficulties are common in students and, in Chapter 5, that they account for a large proportion of cases of academic difficulty. However, by no means every psychiatric casualty is also an academic casualty and it is obviously important to investigate further the nature of the association between the two.

This association is a complex and inadequately explored one. Certainly no simple classification of psychiatric disorder by diagnosis or by severity can adequately account for who does and who doesn't experience academic problems. Even psychotic illness is no absolute bar to academic success, while at the other extreme quite minor neurotic problems may totally inhibit work.

OVERALL CLASSIFICATION

In comparing student psychiatric patients who were working satisfactorily with those who were not, I was unable to distinguish any features or background factors which discriminated between the two groups, with the exception of the tendency for the more severe and particularly psychotic disorders to be accompanied by academic difficulty.[49] Within the group of psychiatric patients in academic difficulty, however, a subdivision of practical use can be made between what one can call the disorganized and the dynamic. Patients in the former group are suffering from a general mental or emotional disturbance which impairs some psychological function essential for successful work, such as memory, concentration, capacity for organization or motivation. The student working under pressure cannot cope with serious impairment in any one of these areas. In the second (dynamic) group, one finds students with a more focal disturbance; they are often coping adequately with most aspects of their lives, but they have neurotic conflicts which are specifically linked in some way with their role of student. Some two to four per cent of all students may, at some stage in their careers, be numbered among the first (disorganized) group and a rather larger proportion among the second. This first group will be only briefly discussed here, as some of the cases described in earlier chapters fall into this category. The dynamic group deserve further attention, not simply because of their greater numbers, but because the mechanisms apparent in these students are probably operative to a lesser degree in many others less obviously incapacitated, and hence an understanding of this group has implications for the whole of teaching.

WORK DIFFICULTY DUE TO ILLNESS – THE DISORGANIZED GROUP

The case histories and descriptions of illness given in preceding chapters will have made it clear that the thought disorder of the schizophrenic, the distractability of the hypomanic, the despair or lack of energy of the depressive, the repetition and perfectionism of the obsessional and the preoccupation of the severely anxious may all constitute non-specific assaults upon the student's academic capacity. For the student disabled in this way, work represents an unattainable goal or an irrelevant distraction, and a period of absence from study is essential. The role of a university health service in such a case, as in the case of physical illness, is to arrange treatment, to maintain contact and to ensure adequate recovery before return. We do not, unfortunately, enjoy central psychiatric facilities for students such as are provided for the treatment of such cases in France. We must therefore rely upon the scattered and uneven facilities of the National Health Service which makes it extremely difficult to reintroduce study gradually during hospitalization. Once patients who have needed absence for this type of illness return to the university, it is important to maintain medical supervision and to advise tutors whether full academic pressures should be applied.

WORK DIFFICULTY DUE TO NEUROTIC CONFLICT – THE DYNAMIC GROUP

As indicated above, the students in this group are less obviously ill and are consequently likely to provoke a less sympathetic and understanding response from their tutors. The actual response given by a tutor, whether authoritarian ('produce this essay, pass this test or get out') or permissive ('well old chap you are obviously in a bit of a state, don't worry about those essays you owe me this week') often reflects the tutor's personality and values more than the individual student's needs. The more sophisticated tutor may make the distinction between well and responsible for his actions (therefore lazy and needing pressure) and ill and not responsible (therefore needing sympathy and support), but in my view, these variations in response need to be further elaborated. The model for the interaction between student and tutor needs to take account of the unconscious, irrational components which are explicable in psychodynamic terms.

The Irrational Transaction Between Tutor and Student

To understand another individual, one has to gauge the way in which the world looks from where he is; indeed, it is only to the extent that we can achieve this that we can communicate. The point is well made in a play by Pirandello.[44]

LAUDISI: ... I find you all anxiously trying to search out who other people are, and what things are really like. ... Just as if people and things were like this or like that, simply because they are what they are.

MRS SIRELLI: According to you, then, we can *never* know the truth?

MRS CINI: Things have come to a pretty pass if we're no longer to believe in what we can see and touch!

LAUDISI: Oh yes, dear lady, you must believe . . .! However, let me urge you to respect what others see and touch, even if it is the exact opposite of what you yourself see and touch . . .

The tutor who can only explain a student's work difficulty in terms of laziness or illness may be failing to appreciate how he himself, the university or the work may look from the student's position; he may be failing to respect what students 'see and touch'. To learn to appreciate this he may need to borrow some of the psychotherapist's skills. The therapist has to learn to watch for the hidden assumptions beneath the surface of what the patient says and to be alert to what the patient does not say so that he can build up a picture of the structure of expectations and fantasies which constitutes the patient's world view. The tutor who finds himself faced with a student who has an academic problem which fails to respond to reasonable or common sense remedies does not need to become a therapist; but he can learn to listen in a similar way for signs of the underlying difficulties which may exist between himself and the student, and to recognize the operation of unconscious processes. In particular, he can learn to avoid the trap set for him by the neurotic student, who invites him to play one of the ready-made parts in the neurotic fantasy repertoire (good mother, authoritarian father or whatever) rather than to continue in his proper role of tutor. An understanding of the possibility of irrational transactions of this sort strengthens the tutor's capacity to anchor his relationship in the reality situation of being tutor to a student, and diminishes the danger that he will find himself colluding in such transactions and the resulting role confusion.

The rest of this chapter will be devoted to illustrating some of the ways in which neurotic problems in the student may block his capacity to work. These illustrations present psychodynamic explanations of neurotic work difficulty. In addition, to illustrate these explanations, I have given the results of Repertory Grid Testing, as this technique offers an objective display of the processes described by psychodynamic formulations, and thus cannot simply be dismissed as the fantasies of the therapist involved (in these cases myself).

REPERTORY GRID TESTING

The aim of Repertory Grid Testing is to establish the subject's view of himself and of those around him. Details of the method and of the underlying theory of personal constructs, as originated by Kelly[28] and developed by others[2, 3, 52], are described in a number of publications. The subject himself supplies the names of people to be included in the test, although the tester can specify certain significant individuals, such as parents, or certain categories such as teachers. The tester then talks about these people (called the elements) with the subject, getting him to compare and contrast them and noting down the descriptions used and the feelings expressed. The test is carried out by listing all the descriptions (called the constructs) which the subject has supplied and asking the subject to indicate how far each construct is a true or false description of each person on the list. This is usually done by means of a 5 or 7 point rating scale. The completed test consists, therefore, of a grid or matrix of ratings representing the subject's own judgements of people he had chosen in his own terms. To complete the test the subject must decide, for example, that John is more trustworthy than Alan but less so than James, or that James is more intelligent than John, while John is more intelligent than Alan; that is to say he must make the type of comparative judgement that one does make, consciously or unconsciously, in one's day-to-day contacts with other people.

Analysis of this matrix in my cases was carried out by means of the computer programme of Dr Patrick Slater of the Institute of Psychiatry. This analysis enables one to explore a number of areas of psychological interest. For one thing, one can see how two different constructs are related for a given subject, for example: are ambitious people seen by him as cold, or are blondes seen as preferable? The degree of association between ambitious and cold or between blonde and preferable can be expressed as a correlation ranging from minus 1 which means that the descriptions are opposite in meaning for the subject, through 0 which means that they are unrelated, to plus 1 which means that the two constructs are virtually identical in their significance for him. The computer programme also extracts from the grid what are called principal components. These are mathematical abstractions which can be taken to represent the main underlying psychological dimensions of the subject's judgements. The meaning of these components can be deduced by seeing which constructs have the highest loadings, positive and negative, upon them but, strictly speaking, these constructs do not label or define the components. In most cases they turn out to deal with judgements like nice versus nasty or strong versus weak. One can then go on to see where all the significant persons (elements) are placed in relation to these components; in other words, one is able to map out some of the basic structure of the subject's interpersonal perceptions.

In the case histories which follow, references will be made to correlations between constructs; the location of the people (elements) in terms of the first and second principal components will be displayed in the figures. In these figures the components are labelled at either end with those constructs having the highest loadings upon them. The figures therefore provide a summary of how the subject feels about himself and about other important people. This summary will be related to the clinical history.

In the following five case histories of students presenting with serious academic difficulty, the academic record will be given followed by a brief clinical (psychodynamic) assessment and by the results of Repertory Grid Testing. They are simplified and modified to preserve the anonymity of the subjects.

Case 1 N.G. – Male Science Student

Problem – Conflict of motivation; denial mechanisms.

Academic History – This student had an adequate school record, having passed his exams after last-minute panic revision. His academic record at university showed deterioration from the end of his first year, and he was under formal threat of being sent down from the third term of his second year. He evaded this fate narrowly and proceeded to take and fail Finals, observing afterwards that, had he only done four weeks' revision rather than two he might have made it, and feeling rather hard done by that he was not permitted to resit the examination.

Clinical History – This student presented with gastro-intestinal psychosomatic symptoms during his second year. Early in his third year he consulted, asking for advice about his work difficulty. He described a stable parental marriage, a neurotic mother and a fairly uneventful and secure childhood as the only child in the family. He expressed the desire to get a degree, but described his motivation for a career vaguely while he went on to talk about his hobbies with far more enthusiasm. Work was boring and he was soon discouraged by difficulty. At seminars or lectures he would daydream or doze. He denied any major mood disturbance though complaining of some tension, and he continued to have some somatic symptoms. He was not considered to be accessible for psychiatric treatment and his tutors were encouraged to apply firm pressures. The lack of effective anxiety and his capacity to believe that he would get a degree without working suggest the operation of neurotic denial mechanisms, with some physical expression of underlying anxiety.

Repertory Grid Testing – Figure 1 gives the distribution of people in terms of the first two components. In this and subsequent figures, ST stands for school teacher, T for tutor and P for peer-group friend. Women are marked O and men X. GF and BF are past or present girl or boy friends. Parents, grandparents and brothers and sisters are labelled. It is seen in this case that on the first (horizontal) component the father, the Dean (T2) an admired tutor (T1) and the ideal self are on the left, which means here that they tend to be seen as approachable, conventional and pleasant, in contrast to the patient and his peer-group friends on the right who tend to be seen as insecure, neurotic, extraverted and cynical. Friends and the ideal self are towards the top (cynical, admired, extraverted and vigorous) – two tutors, the school teacher, mother and her parents are at the bottom (conventional, not self-aware, drips). Looking at construct correlations it emerges that the construct

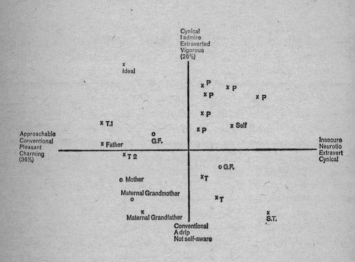

'I like' and the construct 'has the qualities of a good scientist' have a positive correlation of only 0·060; that is to say they are virtually unrelated.

It seems likely that this student was unable to make a successful identification with his father or with the respected teachers who were associated in his mind with his father. One can speculate that this may be because of repressed hostility towards his father and this unexpressed emotion may also have been responsible for his somatic symptoms. This identification problem could also account for the very small number of females included – an unusual feature for the modern student!

His failure in work may have represented an expression of his unacknowledged hostility, buttressed by the fact that, in seeing himself as one of a group of peers whom he contrasted with the adult and academic world, he was making an essentially anti-academic identification.

Case 2 F.G. – Female Arts Student

Problem – Work difficulty compounded of passive resistance and perfectionism based upon an ambivalent relationship with her father.

Academic History – After an adequate school career this student worked poorly throughout her first two years at university. She was consistently late in handing in work, missed tutorials and did poorly in examinations. One important aspect of her work problem was her unwillingness to hand in anything which she regarded as incomplete or of an inadequate standard. As a result of her persistent failure she was placed at the beginning of her third year on the Vice-Chancellor's list (i.e. warned that she must work better or be sent down).

Clinical Evaluation – F.G. was the youngest of four children. She described her mother as over-anxious and fussy and her father as a demanding, disappointed and dyspeptic man. Neither parent had had higher education, but all four children had got to university and the father placed a very high value upon their achievement. This high demand was incessantly reinforced throughout their school careers and had produced rebellious behaviour in F.G.'s brother and sisters. During her adolescence her father, and later her mother, had been ill and consequently dependent upon her as her siblings had by this time left home. Perhaps for this reason, F.G. herself had remained a compliant, dutiful daughter and was still filled with guilt and anxiety whenever she did not do well. In this case the problem with giving work to tutors seems to have represented a repetition of a problem with her father. At one level she wanted their praise for good work, whereas at another level she resented the degree

to which she had to earn acceptance in this way and resisted
passively the demands made upon her. She had a brief period
in treatment during her third year (after being placed upon the
Vice-Chancellor's list) and seemed to gain some insight. She
became more able to hand in imperfect work and less anxious
about the possibility of getting an indifferent degree, but it
seems probable that her basic conflict remained unresolved.
She graduated with a Lower Second.

Repertory Grid Testing – The distribution of people in terms of
the first two principal components are given in Figure 2. On

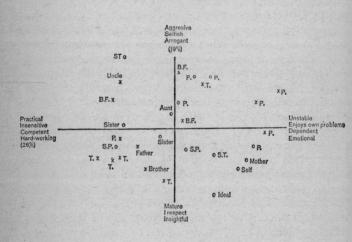

the right one finds the patient, her peer-group friends, her
mother and her ideal self; on the left are her father, brother,
sisters and older family members and also a group of tutors.
Those on the right tend to be seen as unstable and dependent,
those on the left as practical and insensitive. As regards con-

struct correlations, it is of interest that the construct 'warm' had a negative correlation with academic (– ·101) and with hard-working (– ·122). Interpreting this grid it seems that the distribution of elements confirms the clinical conviction that her attitudes to tutors were a reflection of her attitude to her father. The test further highlights a conflict between her wish to succeed and her identification with her mother or, more generally, a conflict between academic and feminine characteristics.

Case 3 N.I. – Male Arts Student

Problem – Compulsive defiance on the basis of an unresolved Oedipal problem.

Academic History – This student had a successful school career with good 'O' and 'A' level passes despite some disciplinary problems at his junior and grammar schools. At university he had recurrent disciplinary problems and from the start his work output was marginal. In his second year, he was given a formal warning that failure to work more consistently would lead to expulsion. Following further disciplinary troubles and a diminished work output, he was sent down in his third year.

Clinical Evaluation – Half-way through his second year, he presented saying that he would like to know why he was unable to meet what he conceded to be the university's reasonable demands. He was the second son of a successful, self-made business man and a professional woman. He saw his parents' marriage as being held together by his mother's tolerance and submission. He himself had a congenital hip dislocation in infancy and was left with a minor degree of shortening in one leg. His elder brother had recently completed a brilliant academic career at another university. Both boys had had major rows with the father during adolescence. During his pre-university years, the patient had lived away from home part of the time and had moved in a beatnik, drug-taking culture. The work problem in this case seemed to result from his need to defy and resist demands made upon him. Achievement, though admired and respected in his father and in one sense sought after, also represented capitulation. An underlying sense of inferiority, perhaps heightened by his minor physical deformity and by a need to compete with his successful brother, was compensated for by the assumption of an attitude of disdain and contempt for others, students and tutors alike. This was expressed particularly in his rudeness and his refusal to work. In his relationship to girls he was overbearing and exploitive, repeating the pattern he described between his parents. He attended only three times and then broke off treatment.

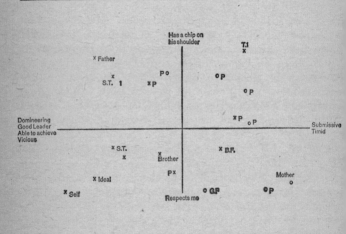

Repertory Grid Testing (Figure 3) – Those on the left are domineering, good leaders, those on the right submissive and timid. Those on top have a chip on their shoulders and are vicious, those below respect him.

There is an unusually marked polarization of men from women, the latter tending to the right, and his mother and his girl friend are seen close together in the bottom right corner as suitably submissive and respectful. The self slightly exceeds the father in strength, but he and his father are polarized on the second component. There is a close matching of self and ideal-self (a sign, incidentally, that treatment is unlikely to be effec-tive). It is noteworthy that a hated teacher (ST1) is construed as very like father, and a hated tutor (T1) is seen as nastier than father, but also weaker.

These findings seem to fit in with the clinical hypothesis. In psychodynamic terms he is probably denying those aspects of himself which are weak or nasty and projecting them on to his father and hated teachers. This being so, academic success (in so far as it implies acceptance of, and perhaps identification with, such teachers) represents an unacceptable threat to his self-concept.

(Note – The friend labelled B.F. is the subject described below as Case 4.)

Case 4 – B.F. – Male Arts Student

Problem – Passive resistance on the basis of unresolved Oedipal problems.

Academic History – After a reasonably satisfactory school career marked by successful pre-examination panic revision, this student obtained a university place on the basis of three 'A' levels (two Bs and a C). During his second year he persistently failed to produce essays, attend tutorials, or answer summonses to explain himself, and he was formally warned that he would be sent down if his work did not improve. At the same time he was advised to consult the health service. Quite soon after this his work improved and he went on, with occasional lapses, to take Finals from which he obtained a lower second degree.

Clinical Evaluation – He presented, on his tutor's advice, dur-ing his second year. He was the younger of two sons, the other brother being ten years older and heartily disliked by the patient. He described his father as an irascible, controlling and unhappy man – the manager of a large business; and his mother as a fussy, anxious and over-protective woman. Both father and the disliked brother were highly achievement-oriented. B.F. reached puberty late. Early in his teens he was much upset when, following a misdemeanour on his part, his father was very angry and was then taken ill with a haemorrhage from a duodenal ulcer. He presented as a somewhat diffident and passive character, but there were no marked problems in his other relationships with men or women, so that his work difficulty appeared as a relatively isolated problem. These difficulties seem to represent a passive refusal to comply with the demands. It was thought that they stemmed from guilt over his father's illness which had prevented a direct adolescent revolt. He was able to express some hostility to the older brother which may have been displaced from the father. His performance improved after he had been seen three times, whether due to the university's formal warning or to the interpretations offered, or to both or neither, cannot be determined.

Repertory Grid Testing (Figure 4) – Those seen as sincere, admired and with integrity are on the left, those distrusted are on the right. Good leaders (who are dominating and make him insecure) are above, contrasted with the dependent, submissive, sensitive below. The construct 'likely to achieve academically' had positive correlations with creative (·80) and with 'I could take my troubles to' (·53) but negative correlations with affectionate (– ·30) and generous (– ·30). B.F. sees himself as the weakest and, by a small margin, the nicest member of his family. N.I. (Case 3 above) is seen as relatively strong and distrusted; he closely resembles the disliked elder brother. N.I.'s girl friend P1 is seen as relatively weak and distrusted. It seems likely that B.F. suppresses his own capacity to be strong or vicious and uses indirect, passive forms of resistance himself, as in his work failure. The only teacher he includes in the test, one from school, has one of the highest loadings for weakness (and presumably therefore constituted no threat). The negative correlation found between academic success and generosity and affection would be likely to inhibit wholehearted striving for achievement even if the passive resistive element in his work troubles were to be overcome.

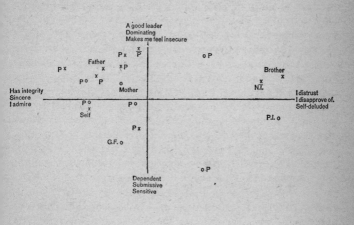

Case 5 N.V. – Female Certificate of Education Student

Problem – Identity problem relating to sex and professional roles.

Academic History – This student had a grammar school education, followed by an adequate but not brilliant Oxbridge career. She ran into difficulties in her Certificate of Education course in her dealings with both fellow teachers and children. She finally left without completing the course.

Clinical Evaluation – N.V. consulted at the suggestion of her supervisor and was in psychotherapy for six months. She was the youngest of three daughters, and 'should have been a boy'.

She described her parents as a restricted, neurotic couple who were not very happy together. Her father had a close, very dependent relationship with his own mother who dominated the family. The father was also close to the patient, particularly in her early years when he involved her in many, largely boyish, activities. From puberty onwards, N.V. exhibited persistent eating problems (food refusal, vomiting) and she remained underweight and she still had difficulty in eating in company. She described her previous boy friends as either wet and useless and unattractive, or as attractive and exploitive. She became over-involved with her supervisor, tended to over-identify herself with the children in opposition to other teachers, and she had become resentful of the demands made upon her. In view of all this it is not surprising that her decision to withdraw from the course was not resisted. In her social life she showed during her period in treatment some increased capacity to relate to men in a less polarized way. In her transference relationship in therapy, she exhibited anger, sexuality, a fear of dependence, a fear of exposure and of being invaded, and marked depression. She ended treatment before she withdrew from the university, saying 'I will only have to separate in the end, so why not now'.

Repertory Grid Testing (Figure 5) – N.V. places herself close to her parents in the top left quadrant, as wet, unsure of self, dependent, anger-arousing, disliked and demanding. Her sisters, two teachers and her ideal self are on the right, as people to whom one can take troubles, sympathetic, sexy and able to achieve. Two ex-boy friends are low down (good leader, authoritarian and aggressive) and one is above father (wet and unsure). The supervisor with whom she had difficulty (T1) is close to the self.

This confirms the tendency to polarize men and the extreme position of the mother and paternal grandmother (on the left) in contrast to the teachers and sisters (on the right) suggests that her own sexual identification may be based upon an unresolved splitting, so that her own 'good femininity' is construed as absent or inaccessible. Men are either weak like father or strong and dangerous. Her difficulties with the supervisor (T1) were probably related to projective mechanisms, that is, she could not cope in relation to him because he represented parts of herself. The difficulty with her pupils was presumably due to the same mechanism and to a lack of confidence in her own good nurturant side. The constructs 'makes me angry' and 'is demanding' had a positive correlation of ·93, so it is scarcely surprising that she experienced some difficulty in being an effective teacher!

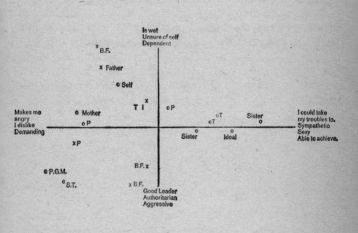

DISCUSSION

These case histories are examples of common neurotic work problems; they do not, of course, constitute a comprehensive view of the psychodynamics of each case. The aim of presenting them is to indicate the complexity of the factors which may underlie such difficulty.

T–D

It is not suggested that the tutor, in the course of his teaching contact, can hope to make individual assessments of his students at this level. But he should be aware of what may be going on and should be prepared and able to refer students with academic problems for psychiatric assessment, even in the absence of obvious psychiatric illness. The tutor who becomes sensitive to what he may mean to the student in fantasy terms and who is alerted to the irrational aspects of the teaching relationship may come to recognize more and more the common patterns responsible for teaching and learning difficulties. He may also have to come to terms with hitherto unrecognized aspects of himself which contribute to these difficulties.

As for the student in difficulty, I hope that these illustrations may help him see how emotional and personality factors, of which he may be unaware, can interfere with his conscious intentions and block the full use of his capacities.

9   Examination Reactions

Examination reactions (stress, panic and phobia) occupy a large place in the mythology of student psychiatry. The reason for this may be that to fail or make a mess of an examination is a piece of student behaviour which cannot escape notice or comment, in the same way as a suicide makes it impossible to evade the reality of a preceding despair or illness. The attention given to suicide and examination reactions is disproportionate and inadequate in that no attention is given to their antecedent causes. In the case of suicide, this can lead to distressingly limited proposals for preventive actions. In the case of examination problems it can lead to proposals to eliminate either examinations or anxious students.

It will be clear from earlier chapters that psychiatric and emotional problems are common and are frequently linked in subtle ways with various aspects of the learning process. Problems which are particularly related to examinations will differ from other work problems only in so far as examinations, especially Finals, take on particular meanings for the individual student. Before looking at what these meanings may be, we should note what the purpose of the examination is in terms of the university and of society. In the eyes of society as a whole, a graduate is someone who has acquired a particular range of skills, and society, especially in so far as it pays for the universities, expects some kind of assurance that these skills have been acquired. The Final examination is a convenient, traditional and relatively economical way of testing this. In addition in Britain, though not in most other countries, it provides one more opportunity of grading and classifying people. This classification, originally, I believe, designed to determine differential pay rates for teachers, provides a last opportunity for the British educational system to define most people as relative failures (e.g. 'good' Honours, and hence, by implication 'poor' Honours).

Examinations, however, have other important functions. Through them teachers can get some idea of how successfully they have taught. Experiments have been tried in which failure of more than a very small proportion of a class led to repetition of the course with new methods or new teachers. Thus the course and not the student was deemed to have failed. Examinations also provide the student with some measure of his performance (though to be effective as an aid to learning, results in this case need to be fed back promptly) and they do, of course, undoubtedly provide an incentive for work, though not always of the most meaningful or effective kind.

There is one other feature of the Finals examination which needs to be noted – its ritual aspect. In the fear, sense of persecution and exhaustion it imposes on many students and in the subsequent ceremonial acceptance into the graduate community, which is acted out on Graduation Day, are shades of other, more primitive, *rites de passage*.

In summary, then, the main functions of examinations are that they test ability for society, for the teacher and for the student, they provide an incentive to work for the student, and they are a rite of transition. In some form or other these functions must be met; but could their present form be altered in such a way as to reduce the ill-effects often attributed to the examination system? And what can exams often mean for the student?

NORMAL PRE-EXAMINATION STRESS

In any testing situation some anxiety is normal; the level of anxiety in a given student will vary according to what is invested in the examination. The very bright scholar, anxious to get a research grant, may be more anxious than the mediocre plodder who will be grateful to get the third class degree which has been predicted for him. The only child, whose father had dropped out of college due to financial difficulties, has different things at stake when he takes Finals than has the wealthy, eldest son, who in any case is going into the family business. The effect of anxiety is also different in different temperaments. The stable, unimaginative, rugger-playing extravert may be stirred to unprecedented cerebral feats as Finals approach, while the tense, ambitious or obsessionally meticulous student may be paralysed by the time pressure and by the importance of the goals at stake. Even in the absence of specific neurotic problems these variations in temperament and in subjective meaning are likely to influence performance considerably so that the examination is to an extent a test of qualities unrelated to academic ability.

In most normally stable students the weeks preceding Finals become dominated by the approaching ordeal. Faculty, formerly amiable, may take on a sinister aspect and their previous kindnesses are seen now as a spider's enticement to the fly. The perception of one's own prospects and skills becomes ludicrously inaccurate. Sometimes an epidemic of anxiety may be triggered off by one disturbed student; in this case, emphatic tutorial and medical intervention is called for, both to help the individual and to protect the others.

During this phase many previously healthy students will consult doctors with sleeping problems – insomnia commonly, but quite often excessive sleepiness, which represents a kind of 'frozen rabbit' opting out of horrid reality. Most of these consulters will be adequately helped with brief support and perhaps sedation for a few days. Where the psychiatric service is functioning well with good tutorial links, very few serious psychiatric problems will first present medically at this stage.

PSYCHIATRICALLY VULNERABLE STUDENTS AT FINALS

Among psychiatric patients examinations can assume all kinds of significance; as threatening exposure of their limitations, or as raising vast existential issues to do with freedom, individuality, 'selling out to the system' and so on. The student who has had or is having treatment can usually be helped to face this reality. The very name Finals brings to some a note of doom, spelling out the end of a phase, the loss of a transitional identity and the beginning of a new and harsher demand from society for commitment and choice. None of these larger issues which become linked on to the commoner examination reactions can be dealt with adequately if they first reveal themselves in the heat of battle. A successful university health service hopefully will have dealt with the majority of such problems during the preceding three years, and major breakdowns interfering with Finals should be a rarity, although some are bound to occur.

EXAMINATION PANIC AND PHOBIA

Panic during examinations or a paralysing terror leading to phobic avoidance of the examination hall has been well described by Malleson.[40] It tends to occur in those who have evaded facing the approaching reality by using denial mechanisms so that they are overwhelmed when the situation is finally forced upon them. The great majority so affected are bright students with no realistic academic cause for anxiety. When a reaction of this type occurs on the eve of, or during Finals, management must be firm and immediate. The student may be helped by being encouraged to experience, by mental rehearsal, the feared situation, while being given the support and reassurance of the doctor. Such rehearsals, carried out under supervision in a state of complete physical relaxation, can help the student experience and cope with his anxiety rather than use ostrich-like evasions; the more he can face anxiety in advance (and the doctor can help here by spelling out the nature of the ordeal to come and the consequences of failure) the less likely he is to be overwhelmed in the examination hall. For these students, and for some psychiatric patients known in advance to be at risk, the provision of a 'sheltered workshop' in which to take Finals can be of great assistance. This should consist of a quiet room attached if possible to the Health Centre, with its own invigilator, where coffee, encouragement, nursing and medical support are available. A few students may even need to take their papers in the Health Centre sick bay for either medical or psychiatric reasons. Admission to the 'sheltered workshop' should be by medical recommendation, but tutors and invigilators should all be made aware of the facilities and how to apply to the doctor for admission. In my experience up to five per cent of students may use such facilities most for only a small part of the examination. The fears of tutors who have the fantasy that only a minority would take Finals in the examination halls can therefore be allayed.

SHOULD THE SYSTEM BE CHANGED?

With the medical service working well in close contact with tutors throughout the student's years at university, and providing special support over Finals, as outlined above, the number of Finals casualties should be extremely small. In my experience at Sussex only about one per cent of students embarking upon Finals fail to complete enough papers to be eligible for a class degree, but higher rates are reported from some universities. But even if this low rate were general, one might still ask whether the survival of this particular ordeal is a good measure of ability or of relevant character traits. However, any alternative system of examining is likely to produce its own crop of casualties and its own varieties of stress. The solution seems to be to introduce a far greater flexibility and variety into the methods of testing used, so that individuals handicapped under one particular set of conditions have the opportunity to show their powers in a different testing situation. One cannot make an initial selection of students simply in terms of those who will succeed in one particular form of examination; each university must therefore endeavour to provide for students of widely differing temperaments the opportunity to give the best possible account of themselves. In practice this could be achieved by relying upon a range of assessments for each subject being examined. Some weight could be given for course work, without necessarily going as far as the American system of course credits. Formal examinations during and at the end of the course could include project work, dissertations and extended essays to a greater extent so that memory and speed would be less crucial to success than they are in the present standard three-hour feats of memory, endurance, and (to be generous) of synthetic thinking ability. Even the fairest method of assessment will still produce stress because students have a human desire to do well and a human fear of failure. However, the change to more flexible methods, with more emphasis on dissertation seems, on brief experience at Sussex, to have been accompanied by both educational advantages and a diminished incidence of health problems.

10   Suicide and Self-Injury

Successful suicide and acts of self-injury or poisoning are both more common among students than among others.[56] The national rate for the age-group runs at about four per 100,000 per year. Figures from universities are very variable, but the red brick and older universities report rates about three to five times higher, while Oxford and Cambridge have rates nearly seven to ten times higher than this figure.[6] The explanation for this high general rate and for the even higher Oxbridge rates is not clear. One can point to the various stresses of student life, to the high proportion of overseas and hence up-rooted people, to examinations, to the loss of status involved in failure and to the fragmented and isolated social circumstances of many students, but any rigorous assessment of the importance of each of these factors is lacking.

In the general population a large proportion of successful suicides occur in that group of people who are suffering from depressive illnesses (manic-depressive psychosis). This condition accounts for many student suicides also, but other conditions are probably more common in the student age-group, and quite a number of student suicides occur in people with no known history of preceding mental illness. Student suicides may occur at any time in the student's career, but figures for students share the national tendency to a higher rate in the spring.

ATTEMPT OR GESTURE?

Non-fatal suicidal acts, mainly involving only slight risks to life, are common and are becoming increasingly so. People who attempt suicide and those who succeed form two largely separate populations with only a small overlap. Some of this overlap is due to the fact that the individual with serious suicidal intent may fail on his first attempt. It is therefore important *never* to dismiss an unsuccessful attempt as 'unreal' without determining how large a risk to life there was, what precautions were taken to avoid discovery, and what, if anything, was left in the way of a suicide note; this assessment must, of course, be combined with a careful psychiatric diagnosis. Most of those who make suicidal attempts, however, expose themselves to very little risk, at most to a gambler's chance of death. Some of the overlap is accounted for by the occasions when these gambles do not come off. If the problem underlying the suicidal gesture is not resolved, however, further attempts at shorter odds may be taken. Of those who make more than one such attempt, about one in twenty go on finally to kill themselves.

The majority of acts of self-injury or poisoning are therefore not so much attempts at self-destruction as statements and communications. As such, none should be disregarded any more than should the direct voicing of a suicidal intent. To injure oneself, even without immediate fatal intent, is an expression of hopelessness or anger and, implicitly or explicitly, a plea or a demand for more support.

Some individuals may use threats or suicide bids as a transparent attempt to exert control over others. The others in these cases are commonly boy or girl friends, although patients in psychotherapy will often use this weapon against their doctors. But such tactics spring from a lack of trust in self or others and it is to this underlying lack of trust and to the cry for help that the response must be directed.

DANGER SIGNALS

From what has been said, it is clear that every threat and every attempt is a danger signal, and those around should seek medical advice, irrespective of the wishes expressed by the individual. This can pose a difficult choice for the friends of a depressed student who specifically asks that nobody is informed of his state; but false loyalty here can be fatal. A depressed person is not able to weigh up the prospects of change and recovery or the possibility of help. His perception of others may be distorted by his depression, or he may be striving unconsciously to prove that others do not care, and in effect challenges them to show that they do not. The strain such a person puts upon his friends is considerable and they should use what advice and help doctors can offer. In many such cases the doctor may be able to make some assessment without seeing the depressed person or to suggest ways in which he may be persuaded to consult.

While threats or attempts at suicide provide certain warning of risk, not every successful suicide is heralded by evidence of this kind, and if prevention of suicide is to be really adequate there must be an early recognition and referral to a doctor of anyone with serious psychiatric disorder, especially depression. The friend or the tutor who notices in a student a change in personality with, for example, loss of interest in his work, in himself, or his friends, marked mood swings, increased alcohol intake or complaints of persistent sleep difficulty should advise and if necessary provoke a consultation.

CERTIFICATION

Compulsory admission to hospital under certificate is very rarely required. When it is required it tends to be seen by students as an authoritarian and impermissible move. There are, however, times when any other course of action would constitute either a lack of concern or a lack of judgement. Even patients in psychotherapy can usually accept in retrospect their therapist's decision to hospitalize them over suicidal phases, seeing this as care rather than oppression, or as a doctor's only possible course in the face of the threats issued.

PREVENTION

Suicide provides the one incontrovertible piece of evidence of mental distress. To reduce its incidence demands a sensitivity to the whole range of difficulties that may precede or signal its approach. Individuals and institutions, including universities, are still capable of incomprehension and prejudice to an extraordinary degree in their attitude to emotional problems and psychiatric illness. There is a widespread fantasy that offering support to vulnerable people undermines their strength, an attitude which underestimates the understanding of doctors and ignores the nature of illness. I am reminded of an occasion upon which I was defending psychotherapy to a group of academics; my most effectively persuasive argument was to point out that the process often involves the patient in considerable emotional pain. On this basis it was much more acceptable.

There are no short cuts to preventing student suicides; it must involve the university in the creation of a society where individuals are valued in human terms and it demands the provision of adequately staffed medical and psychiatric services.

11 Illegal Drug Use

Addiction to drugs in Britain is a relatively small problem, but one which is slowly increasing. Illegal drug use, on the other hand, has undoubtedly become far more prevalent in the last few years and has, it is believed, achieved particular popularity among students, a phenomenon which follows the transatlantic example. In this chapter I will summarize, briefly, the pharmacological effects of the commonly used drugs and discuss the social and psychological causes and effects of drug use.

DRUG EFFECTS

The effects of drugs, even in rats, vary considerably with the context in which the drug is taken. It is quite clear that this applies to human drug use and that many of the effects attributed to the drugs by illegal drug users are effects produced by the social setting and expectations which go with such illegal drug use. For this reason it is never safe to generalize too firmly about the pharmacological effects of any given substance. However, as a preamble to this chapter I will summarize the typical pharmacological effects of the commonly-used illegal drugs.

Amphetamines

Amphetamines taken alone or in combination with barbiturates were the first illegal drugs to be widely circulated in Britain and they are also widely prescribed, despite much medical opinion which regards their use with disfavour under almost all circumstances. The main effect of amphetamines is to inhibit fatigue and appetite and to produce a euphoric state of mind. In small doses they have long been favoured by students as a means of overcoming fatigue while completing the next morning's essay, or engaging in a work binge to compensate for previous indolence or distraction. At the cost of some sacrifice in accuracy they are relatively effective for this purpose, although there is often a subsequent swing into lethargy and depression. But they are only effective for short-term postponement of fatigue, and if taken for more than one or two days in succession the total output of work will fall to the individual's usual level. Regular dependence on the drug for help over crises can lead to eventual habituation and addiction.

The cult user of amphetamines takes much larger doses, usually to enable him to keep going for a weekend of frenetic sociability. Used in this high dosage amphetamines are rapidly addictive for some individuals and a small number of high dosage users will develop a psychotic illness resembling schizophrenia. Delinquency is often associated with amphetamine use.

Methedrine is more rapidly acting than the more widespread dextro-amphetamine. Recently, intravenous methedrine has become fashionable in the hard core of drug users; taken in this way it is highly addictive and dangerous, possibly equivalent in risk to heroin.

Cannabis

Cannabis (marijuana, hashish or 'pot') is the most widely favoured illegal drug and is probably the one with least inherent danger. Smoked in the usual way it produces, for most people, a bland somewhat fatuous euphoria and some hallucinatory experience. Under the right circumstances, appreciation of music and other art forms is felt to be heightened. Perception of time is distorted and at least the illusion of a new kind of openness to others is experienced. It produces little in the way of after-effects beyond suffusion of the whites of the eyes (which does not mean to say that every student wearing dark glasses is trying to conceal the fact that he was 'stoned' the night before). There have been fatalities from intravenous use of privately made infusions of cannabis.

LSD ('acid')

LSD is the drug with the most marked pharmacological effects and the one around which the most highly developed mystique has developed. It produces major distortions of perception, of shapes, colours, the subject's body image and the meanings attached to objects, to time and to ideas. Disturbed and dream-like experiences, sometimes with the vivid re-enactment of childhood memories or fantasies, are common. If the 'trip' is a bad one the subject may experience intense fear and may become paranoid. Under these circumstances dangerously violent or omnipotent behaviour may occur. For example, in one case, a student eviscerated his landlady's cat, and destroyed three years' lecture notes belonging to a colleague; in other cases, walking out of upstairs windows, crossing streets with total disregard for traffic and similar behaviour has been reported. In rare cases, a psychotic illness lasting several days or weeks may follow the taking of LSD.

In most subjects the effects of LSD fade away over one to two days and the experience is usually recalled as a powerful one. As the central profundity of the experience appears to be essentially incommunicable, it must be taken on trust. Users of LSD often make large claims for its effects in inducing self-knowledge and a new mode of relating to others and to the world – indeed to the universe. These claims reflect those published by the archpriests of the cult (e.g. Watts)[61] and share with them, besides a certain poetic charm, either impenetrable vagueness about the virtues of the experience described, or an insistence upon the uniqueness of modes of being which are in no sense foreign to those whose brains are biochemically undisturbed. Doubtless the promises held out, strengthened by the ritual aspects of the cult, serve to make the individual's experience of the disturbance in perception and consciousness which the drug provokes into something which can be personally meaningful. Whether subsequent behaviour is more loving, sensitive or creative is less certain – I have not been struck by the evidence for this in the few people I have encountered personally who have undergone the experience of a 'trip'. Moreover, an increasing number of patients have reported the recurrence of LSD type symptoms weeks or months after their last drug use. At times these symptoms can be intense, frightening and recurrent. Both in its short-term and possible long-term effects, LSD is a dangerous drug.

There are a number of other 'psychedelic' drugs, naturally occurring or synthetic, with broadly similar affects to LSD. At the time of writing these are common in the United States of America but are rarely available in Britain.

Opiates (Morphine, Heroin etc.) and Cocaine

Most cult drug users are aware of the dangers of the rapidly addictive opiates, though quite a number have taken them once or twice experimentally and students (or, more commonly, ex-students) are disproportionately represented among the growing number of heroin addicts. Addiction to these drugs, once established, is difficult to treat and the risk of death is much higher than with addiction to other drugs. To embark upon opiates is to embark upon a slow suicide and sometimes there is a conscious awareness and acceptance of this fact.

HOW MANY STUDENTS TAKE DRUGS?

It is extremely difficult to obtain reliable information about the frequency of drug use in universities or elsewhere because of the illegality of the practice and because of the solidarity of the cult members. One of the most convincing journalistic accounts of the drug 'scene' was provided by Fryer[18]. Information which is gathered through university health services is naturally biased in that informants will usually be neurotic individuals seeking treatment, or, in my experience, neurotic individuals referred for treatment following academic failure. Obtaining estimates of prevalence from random questioning of students produces a wide range of estimates due, I suspect, to the relatively closed nature of the drug-taking clique, so that whereas one individual may know a number of drug users, another may have no known contact with any. It is my impression that on the arrival at university, a sizeable proportion of students have already experimented with drugs, particularly, I suspect, those living in certain areas in certain large towns. Within this group there will be a small number of proselytizers, some of whom will have contacts with sources of supply. Around these figures groups will grow up, selected from a much larger range of first-year students who attend one cannabis smoking party or dabble on the margin in some other way. These groups may or may not make contact with existing groups in other years. From what research has been attempted, and from anecdotal evidence, my guess would be that perhaps more than thirty per cent of students, at some time, may take an illegal drug and that up to ten per cent may, at least for a time, take some drug regularly, commonly cannabis. Of this drug-taking tenth, in turn only one in ten will be known to the health service or to the university authorities.

WHAT KIND OF STUDENT TAKES DRUGS?

It is clearly unwise to generalize from the health service sample but it does seem from their evidence that they share characteristics with their non-consulting colleagues, representing only the more extreme cases of a group. Most of those involved are male and, typically, have problems to do with masculinity; they tend to show passive hostility towards authority and to have few or unsatisfactory heterosexual relationships. Their psychopathology is most often related to unresolved Oedipal problems, or to early deprivation.

These problems manifest themselves in the university setting in under-achievement and in that evasion of academic demands which is so characteristic of the 'passive resister'. Work difficulties due to these personality problems may be further exacerbated by the effects of fatigue (drug taking being predominantly nocturnal), and by residual drug effects, leading to failure to attend Monday classes or 9 a.m. lectures, or to the attending of classes while still 'stoned'. The normally capable student who sits glazed or incoherent through a seminar, or whose perform- ance shows marked fluctuations, may be in this last category.

WHAT HAPPENS TO DRUG USERS?

Drug taking and membership of a drug-taking group can fulfil a number of psychological needs for the neurotic individual. The drug itself can relieve tension and anxiety, especially in the case of cannabis, and the group offers non-critical accept- ance and the common pursuit of pleasurable goals. Being part of an illegal peer group can at once constitute an act of rebellion (passive in so far as no direct confrontation with authority need occur) and an act of dependence in that the good group is com- forting and provides a warm balance for the harsh, demanding, unsupportive world outside. This function of the group is perhaps too transparently regressive to be acceptable, but the mystique of drug taking also promises instant insight and instant relationship to members of the cult, an offer most attrac- tive to the individual most uncertain of his identity and most aware of his incapacity to communicate with others. To be an 'acid-head' or a 'pot-head' allows the individual to postpone or evade the assumption of his final identity and his independent coping with reality, by resort to wish-fulfilment fantasies. The slogans and the myths promise new forms of communica- tion and self-awareness, but the experience is increasingly one of pseudo-togetherness, empty of concern or commitment, and of a retreat into the contemplation of a diminishing, impover- ished self.

The majority of drug users, even the more neurotic, on find- ing that the promised rewards of such a cult are temporary or illusory, are able to cut off and to perform the emotional task of taking on the real world and real relationships. For some of these, the temporary experience of belonging to the supportive drug group may have been of benefit, just as a regressive, de- pendent, relationship with an individual may help a deprived person to grow providing he can go on to learn to separate. For others, however, the experience may be harmful. The split between the bad world of reality (characterized by examinations, competition, power and violence which seem to overwhelm the possibility of creativity or love) and the good world of the drug cult (where acceptance and comfort and at least the slogans of creativity are to be found) may reflect, and may come to perpetuate, an inner split in the personality. Such an individual may come to rely more and more on the drug and on the cult, and become less and less a member of the wider society. Often he will act out his hostility towards the wider society and simultaneously maintain his financial stability by becoming a distributor of drugs, and often he will increase the amount of drugs used and the range of drugs with which he experiments. Academic failure is likely to be the first definite sign of impending social breakdown in these cases. This may be staved off for a surprisingly long time, even to the point at which physical deterioration such as weight loss and self-neglect are already apparent. It is from this group, I believe, that the opiate addicts will be recruited. The tragedy of the university drug cult, in my opinion, is not so much that it involves a large number of students in what is largely a fatuous or illusory activity, but that it makes a small number inaccessible to help and condemns some of them to a shortened, destructive and empty existence.

UNIVERSITY POLICY

Drug taking is illegal and is believed to be especially common among students. Universities are therefore bound to adopt some attitude and policy towards it. Doctors, of course, are bound here as elsewhere by confidentiality though there is now a statutory obligation to notify heroin addiction. The choice for the university authorities is basically whether to regard drug taking, if discovered, as a matter for university or for civil action. In my view, the police should be called in if the evidence is good enough for the police and it should be left for the police to act. If the evidence is not good enough for the police then there is no justification for the university to mete out punishments. Where there has been conviction of a student for possession (the only legal offence at present), the university must decide whether any further action should be taken against him. Here there are two considerations: the individual and the community. In any particular case the needs of both must be considered. Unless there is clear evidence that the student has been supplying others and proselytizing, it is my view that the university should leave punishment to the courts and should allow the student to continue with his career, provided he meets normal academic and disciplinary requirements, and possibly provided he accepts additional forms of supervision.

Where a student is failing academically and is receiving treatment in the health service for problems which include drug taking, the medical recommendation will depend upon the use the student is able to make of treatment. In cases where heavy consumption of drugs is a feature, neither teaching nor psychotherapy are likely to get very far, and the student may be best advised to withdraw.

It would be a mistake, however, to regard the treatment of cases or the punishment of transgressors as the only problems which should concern universities. The existence of an oppositional underground culture, however personally disturbed the individuals who are attracted by it, points to a malaise in society. In the world as a whole, and in the university in particular, the philosophy and the existence of the deliberate 'drop-out' is a symptom that should not be ignored. It may be true that the individuals involved have particular problems to do with power and authority or particular incapacities in trusting others, and it may be true they are seeking a magical solution to these problems. But it can also be true that the official values of a world preoccupied with production and achievement, and characterized by massive injustices and violence, are ignoring whole dimensions of human need and experience. If the inhabitants of the drug world are often projecting on to the world a split which arises within them, the world outside may, in its turn, be tending to deny or destroy important aspects of human reality.

The conflict between reason and order on the one hand and feeling and experience on the other is no new problem; it was a major theme of the classical Greek dramatists and their emphasis on the need for a balanced recognition of both forces may be recalled with advantage today. In the *Bacchae* of Euripides it was the failure of Pentheus to give due place and acknowledgement to Dionysus which led to the tragedy.

Student Sex and Student Pregnancy

The sexual behaviour of young people has been subject to a good deal of scrutiny, some of it commendably objective, but much of it uncomprehending and prejudiced. While we now have reasonably accurate knowledge about current behaviour patterns, thanks especially to Schofield's survey,[51] the lack of valid data from previous times makes it difficult to evaluate how major a sexual revolution has in fact occurred. Two factors are likely to lead to inflation when estimating the degree of change, especially in respect of students. The first is the general openness and relative lack of hypocrisy about pre-marital sexual relationships which is now evident. The apparent decrease in chastity may represent, at least in part, a decrease in secretiveness. The second is the increasing proportion of students who are female. The girls with whom male students have affairs, or whom they make pregnant are, nowadays, likely to be fellow-students.

As a dual morality still persists to some extent, evidence of promiscuity on the part of women appears to arouse more anxiety than does that of men. The controversy or outrage provoked by the availability of contraceptive advice at universities, for example, seems basically to be because it makes available effective methods for girls. Men have long since had access to contraception from the chemist or barber's shop.

ARE STUDENTS A SPECIAL CASE?

It is uncertain whether students' sexual behaviour differs from that of their contemporaries. Schofield found that the

university-bound segment of young people of school age were
less sexually active than were their peers. The age range of
students extends into a period at which marriage is relatively
common and it is probably the case that students will tend to
postpone marriage more than their contemporaries. The percentage of girls marrying before the age of twenty in Britain
had reached over twenty per cent in the 1950s but a disproportionate number of these teenage brides were of working-
class origin. It is also the case that a higher proportion of
teenage brides are pregnant at the time of marriage than is the
case with those marrying older; a proportion probably reaching
one in three.[46] It is my impression that students are less likely
to accept a marriage forced by pregnancy and less likely to
become pregnant as a means of forcing parental consent for
marriage, than is the case for the population as a whole. They
also have more obvious reasons for postponing marriage as
most will probably wish to graduate before marrying. For all
these reasons it is likely that among students pre-marital sexual
relationships will seem more prevalent, and less likely that pre-
marital conception will be subsequently legalized by marriage.

WHAT GOES ON IN UNIVERSITIES?

It is likely that a fifth to a third of university students will
already have had a sexual relationship involving intercourse
before arriving at university. The proportion will be rather
higher in the case of men than in the case of women, but the
discrepancy between the sexes is probably less than is the case
in the population as a whole. This estimate is, to an extent,
guesswork, based as it is upon clinical impressions in various
universities and a survey too small to be of significance. It
represents a reasonable extrapolation from Schofield's surveys.
University health services offering contraceptive advice will
find that a small proportion of girls will already have had such
advice before arrival at university (probably something in the
region of three to five per cent). Over the ensuing three years
there will be a steady flow of requests for contraceptive advice,

amounting to about fifteen per cent of the population annually. A further proportion of girl students will obtain advice independently through the youth advisory clinics or other private sources. Pre-marital sexual relationships are therefore presumably experienced by a third to a half of all university women, and probably by a rather higher proportion of men, before graduation.

Despite the availability of contraceptive advice for the unmarried in recent years and despite in particular the student's greater sophistication and willingness to seek such advice, a distressing proportion of women students become pregnant. In the 1960s nearly ten per cent of unmarried women became pregnant over the three-year university course. How this figure compares with the rate in the past is hard to evaluate, for in the last decade the availability of university health services offering treatment has increased, leading to fuller case recording, and the punitiveness of universities and the public in general has diminished. The interpretation of the law permitting therapeutic abortions had also become more liberal in some quarters in the years preceding the 1967 Act. These factors, one suspects, will have led to a reduced concealment of illegitimate pregnancies, whether carried to term or aborted.

Whether or not the sexual problems of university students can be regarded as essentially similar to those of others, these are clearly matters upon which universities must have some information and some attitude. What is the effect of current patterns of sexual behaviour upon the student's academic career, personal stability and development? How far are these the proper concern of the university? What part should a university health service play in giving contraceptive advice? What are the causes for the high pregnancy rate and can any preventive measures be envisaged?

UNIVERSITY ATTITUDES TO STUDENTS' SEXUAL BEHAVIOUR

The first concern of a university is for the student's academic progress; if this is satisfactory it is questionable how far the university is justified in imposing standards of behaviour in other areas. Thinking about this issue is inevitably muddled. Many academics who have a benign, paternalistic concern for the welfare and morals of their students believe that the university should impose controls as a defence for the student against (presumably) bad impulses, or bad company. A larger body of academics would concede that sexual and other private behaviour is the concern of the individual. They would argue that the university should have no concern except in so far as there is an effect on others or on the university. Put brutally, defenders of this view-point would impose sanctions on students only for *blatant* defiance of conventional *mores*. For example, they would forbid open cohabitation, because such behaviour excites adverse comment, magnifies the difficulty of finding student accommodation, and threatens to dry up private bene-factions to the university. A third group of academics would regard this lack of principle as dishonest and unworthy of an institution claiming to be concerned with truth and reason; for those holding this view the universities' principles should be established and then defended even though they may be dis-crepant with public opinion.

In practice the first, paternalistic, view-point is becoming in-creasingly untenable in the face of a host of other cultural factors, which encourage the earlier assumption of personal responsibility; and the third view-point has nowhere been wholeheartedly embraced. In consequence an ambiguous and shifting compromise solution is the norm. While this may be confusing for students. I suspect in fact that peer-group pres-sures are of far greater importance in changing attitudes and determining sexual behaviour than are any official pronounce-ments or regulations, which may indeed be 'counter produc-tive', given the mood of this era and this age-group. Peer-group pressures are probably strong and hard to resist and this is sometimes held to justify the university in maintaining some kind of prohibition as a balancing force. Such regulations, it is argued, impose upon the individual the need to make a direct choice to break a rule, and can provide some kind of external prop for a wavering conscience. But such regulations are virtually unenforceable, and this must undermine much of the effect which is claimed for them.

My own view is that the only direct function of the university in this area should be to provide some sort of access for the student to a member of an older generation so that conformity to peer-group pressures, or defiance of parental or institutional values, are not the sole determinants of behaviour. Such a person might be a tutor, a chaplain, or a doctor, and the student should be able to choose which.

UNIVERSITY HEALTH SERVICE ATTITUDES

One of the main arguments in favour of the provision of contraceptive advice in university health services is that it provides students with an opportunity of discussing the issues presented by sexual relationships in a non-judgemental setting. The emphasis should be upon consultation and not upon slot-machine availability, for this ensures that individuals or couples considering whether or not to embark upon a sexual relationship have a possibility of voicing their doubts and of being confronted with their inconsistencies. I do not personally believe that a doctor should or need refuse contraceptive advice to any individual who firmly decides that he or she wants it, but I do believe that a doctor can help people reach decisions which are thought out and felt out, and are not dominated either by external social or by internal unconscious pressures. In practice, the majority of students consulting for contraceptive advice have already embarked upon a sexual relationship. Most of these have done so after due deliberation, but even where such deliberation has been lacking, there is nothing to be gained, once a pattern of behaviour is established, from depriving the individual of an effective contraceptive method. Faced with the girl who cannot understand, or will not discuss, her sexual behaviour, the doctor is forced into his very traditional role of observing what appears to be human folly, while lacking the brief or the capacity to do very much about altering it.

Effective contraception can only be obtained through doctors, and in this age group, the choice lies between the diaphragm, plus spermicidal jelly, or the pill. The former method has no side-effects of importance but does have a small-percentage chance of the method failing and of conception occurring. This risk can be further reduced by the 'braces and a belt' policy of using a sheath in addition over the probable fertile period (tenth to eighteenth day of a twenty-eight-day cycle). The pill is virtually 100 per cent safe as regards contraception, but it causes minor side-effects and one woman in 2,000 is likely to have a more serious complication, sometimes a fatal one. The choice between these risks and safeties can be left to the patient, except where there are medical contra-indications to the use of the pill. Increasingly, the choice made is for the pill. Either method requires regular specialist medical supervision; this is normally charged for by clinics or private practitioners at the rate of a few pounds per year.

WHAT KIND OF STUDENTS HAVE SEXUAL RELATIONSHIPS?

I am not aware of any published evidence on this matter. My own first impression was that students attending for contraceptive advice were indistinguishable from others in terms of neuroticism, intelligence, attractiveness or any other dimension. To test this, I listed the names of girls who came for contraceptive advice and compared them with a control group who did not. In this study (which can be said to contrast the wise non-virgins with either the virgins or the foolish non-virgins) comparisons were made in terms of personality and intelligence measures tested at intake and in terms of subsequent academic performance. There were no significant differences between the two groups on any criterion.

THE PROBLEM OF PREGNANCY

As stated earlier, availability of contraceptive advice does not eliminate the problem of the unwanted pregnancy, though it may reduce it to below the national rate of approximately ten per cent over the three-year period. The problem of the unwanted pregnancy therefore contributes to the pool of student casualties to quite a marked degree. Some girls arrive at university already pregnant and thereafter there is a continuing rate through the three years. A negligible proportion of these pregnancies result from the failure of a reliable contraceptive technique. Where unreliable methods have been relied upon (for example, coitus interruptus, the 'safe' period, sheath etc.) the individuals have usually been aware that some risk was being incurred. In other cases advice has been obtained but ('just once, doctor') not used. This picture points to only one conclusion; risking pregnancy is at some level a motivated act and even where every conscious, rational intention is to avoid pregnancy, some girls expose themselves repeatedly to this risk and apparently need to do so.

The majority of these girls once faced with an unwanted pregnancy react to it with rejection, anxiety or despair and come to the doctor with a request for termination. Evaluation of this request is a peculiarly difficult task and always a depressing one, for the situation essentially represents a choice between two evils. The doctor's role in these cases must be to attempt to discover the meaning of the pregnancy to the girl, to define the degree and nature of unconscious motivation operating and to uncover her present feelings and her likely future adjustment to either an abortion or a baby. In all cases there are mixed positive and negative feelings towards the pregnancy and there is usually a strong wish to seek a resolution of the conflict by making a definite choice. The girl will attempt to provoke the doctor into making the decision easier, but this attempt should be resisted, and the girl (and where possible her consort) should be helped to deal realistically with the situation and to explore in depth her feelings about it. An automatic readiness to accept at face value a request for termination is, in my view, as much an evasion of responsibility as is an automatic refusal ever to consider it. Termination in these students is very often the right course however much one may regret this necessity. Girls who get pregnant are likely to be neurotic and this neurotic loading is likely to operate increasingly as effective contraception becomes available and reduces the number of pregnancies due to method failures. In such a girl, continuing with an unwanted pregnancy can make resolution of the neurotic problem more difficult, quite apart from the social complications and major emotional problems of coping with the child or, even more, with having to lose the child through adoption. Termination may lead to guilt and can play a part in subsequent neurotic difficulties, as is illustrated in the first case history in Chapter 6, but giving birth to an unwanted child can also cause guilt of quite an equivalent degree.

The motives for pregnancy in these cases (often, as I have said, unconscious ones) can be various. The pregnancy may represent an assertion of femininity, a child stolen from mother, a defiance of the parents or self-punishment. Some such motivation is found in the majority of cases, while the single lapse from grace after a party, or the manipulative pregnancy aimed to force a marriage, account for a very small minority of student pregnancies. The case history below gives an example of the type of mechanism which may be encountered.

Case History

Pauline, a small, vivacious but insecure student of philosophy was first seen in her second term with academic difficulties. It transpired that she was also guilty about and confused by a lesbian relationship which she had formed with a fellow student. In view of her continuing anxiety she was taken on for psychotherapy.

She described her father as a dependent, aggressive, alcoholic and her mother as a 'door mat'. In her relationships with men, Pauline herself alternated between adopting a sisterly nurturant role and being the emotionally exploited and disregarded partner. In the latter case, the men involved nearly always had an existing tie with another girl or sometimes they were married. The pattern here suggested a compulsive re-enactment of the infantile rivalry with her mother for her father – a rivalry confused by her knowledge of her father's infidelities when she was an adolescent.

Her pregnancy was the result of 'deliberate' risk-taking with a partner with whom for the first time she was attempting to combine a sexual and a human relationship. He was himself a vulnerable neurotic man, tied by a hostile dependency to his own mother. He responded to the pregnancy with its implied threat of a commitment to Pauline with anger and disengagement, whereupon she became severely depressed.

After the pregnancy had been terminated on psychiatric grounds, she suffered from a prolonged depressive and guilt reaction. She felt that her one attempt to be a creative woman had failed, although she did not think her decision to have a termination had been an incorrect one.

This case history and chapter will serve to illustrate a more general theme. When a crisis arrives in someone's life, whether this is over a pregnancy or a sexual problem, as is discussed here, or through other types of circumstance – the doctor's role is twofold; as well as giving support through the crisis itself, he must help the patient learn about the things in himself or herself which helped to bring it about. In this way it is hoped that the crisis can be used to develop greater self-understanding and growth, rather than simply becoming a further step in a downward spiral of social and emotional difficulty.

13   A Comment on Student Protest and Politics

It is impossible to write about students at the present time without reference to their political behaviour. Internationally, many of the political movements of 1968 were initiated by students, and in British universities and colleges there is increasing political action on national issues and over local demands for participation in government.

Conflict and disturbance in institutions may light up conflicts and disturbance within vulnerable individuals and this provides a justification for considering the themes of protest and politics in a book on student casualties. To a large extent, however, this chapter should be regarded as a marginal, personal statement rather than as an objective assessment. My consciousness of the fact that the variables about which I am competent to speak – personality and psychiatric disorder – have only tenuous and uncertain relevance to an understanding of student unrest will ensure that this chapter is a short one.

PSYCHIATRIC EXPLANATIONS OF POLITICS

The temptation to explain away student revolt by reference to psychiatric or pseudo-psychiatric factors needs to be resisted. The argument that students are in revolt, adolescents revolt, and therefore the student revolt is an adolescent revolt – is a specious one. The adolescent revolt is a constant, always with us. At any given period of history the incidence and distribution of pathological manifestations of adolescent revolt may be explained in terms of family structure and family stresses, but these factors do not account for short-term historical swings. The homes of the politically apathetic students of the 1950s did not differ radically from the homes of the militant students of the 1960s and the differences in mood and behaviour must be explained in social and political terms.

This argument does not, of course, deny the effect of family background upon an individual's outlook. The staid, respectable, co-operative student politicians and the wild revolutionaries have both taken up positions which are, in part anyway, predictable from their families' social and economic background, although this predictability is lower for students and graduates than for other citizens. But in both groups of students there will be some in whom neurotic, intrapsychic factors have overridden the broader, social ones. In these individuals, a forced identification with authority or a compulsive defiance of it may determine political attitudes more powerfully than cultural factors and certainly more effectively than rational considerations. Thus, in any conservative movement there are people who, by virtue of their backgrounds and personalities, are unable to defy authority or accept change, and in any revolutionary movement there are similarly people who cannot accept authority or endure the *status quo*. This latter factor accounts, no doubt, for the fissile nature of revolutionary movements. The social and political impact of conservatives or of revolutionaries, however, has nothing to do with the psychopathology which may underlie their attitudes. It derives from a coincidence between their personal needs and a wider, socially-determined mood, and this wider mood has social and political causes.

THE ADOLESCENT INVESTMENT IN CHANGE

Conflict between generations has always been a political fact, and the social and political events which determine the preoccupations of a given historical time inevitably reflect back upon the normal adolescent's development, altering the forms by which the transition to adult status is achieved, and determining, to some degree, the issues around which the fight for independence is waged.

The present adolescent generation has been described as the first one to carry strontium in its bones and the implication of this cannot be ignored. It is a fact which, for some, symbolizes a world made one, a world experiencing change at an unprecedented rate and a world where the gap between the potential and the actual quality of human existence is more apparent and where the juxtaposition of complacency and violence is more unforgivable than ever before. The revulsion against this world is manifest not so much in opposition within the society as in a total questioning of it. The purposes and values of society are rejected and the official means of inducing change, even in democratic countries, are too remote to be seen as relevant.

The adolescent, preoccupied with establishing his own identity, encounters a society which offers no certainties for him to accept or reject and no models to follow, and so one which increasingly induces in its members a sense of impotence. The drop-out, the drug cult, and the protest movements, are all comments upon this situation.

CHANGE IN THE UNIVERSITIES

These wider developments inevitably have their effect upon universities. There are in addition two specific roots to the questioning which is beginning to disturb academic peace. The first of these is a diminution in the influence of caste on selection for university places. Students today include many more who are of working-class, technical and managerial family backgrounds. Such students are no longer a minority, to be, as once was the case, quietly absorbed within and soon indistinguishable from the ruling class, but are now a new and fairly distinct group with a variety of social and political traits of their own. The second factor is the growth of the human sciences. By teaching politics, sociology and psychology the universities themselves are initiating, or at least accelerating, a fundamental questioning of social assumptions.

In this context it seems unlikely that hierarchical or authoritarian institutions will survive unchanged, however many ratepayers may threaten to cut the grants of dissident students. The refusal to listen seriously to student demands and the failure to concede them a voice, can only lead to sterile confrontations and conflict. This does not mean that faculty should abandon its claim to authority; teachers have a special responsibility and deserve a special status. The student is a young, inexperienced, transient member of the university's community and the university does not exist solely to meet his needs. Both faculty, and the society which provides the economic basis for the university, have long-term interests, but the student's right to question the methods of faculty, the purposes of the institution and the nature and intentions of the society must be safeguarded on both political and educational grounds. The liberal tradition of the university system must be sustained today precisely by allowing debate and the continuing exchange of opinion to take place, above all over questions relating to the university itself.

Common interests and conflicts of interests exist in every relationship and in every institution. In the mature relationship conflict can be acknowledged and growth can be derived from it. The university can fulfil a critical social role if it can show itself able to be a mature institution, building out of the conflict of generations and of values a society able to encompass both liberty and change.

14 The Place of the Health Service in the University

Only a handful of university health services in Britain have a history longer than thirty years and in this short time they have evolved in function so that the roles now being filled are very different from those initially conceived for them. The two main changes have been, firstly, the move from providing a routine preventive and screening service, towards providing comprehensive services including treatment; and secondly, the growing attention paid to psychiatry. The first of these changes was helped by the introduction of the National Health Service, the second was prompted by the diminishing burden of serious physical disorder, especially tuberculosis, and by the increasing recognition of the size of the psychiatric casualty list. These changes, and the need for the further development of an occupational medical service taking full account of the relationship between psychiatric and academic difficulty, have been documented in a recent report of a sub-committee of the Royal College of Physicians.[47] Students or tutors in any institution of higher education wishing to improve their facilities in this respect will be well advised to consult this report if they wish for expert backing and guidance. Colleges of education are conspicuously deficient in services of this sort, despite the particular importance of psychological stability in the teacher.

My own view of the function of a student health service in the field of mental health will be clear from previous chapters. For the individual student, the service should provide ease of access, confidentiality, and a staff sensitive to psychiatric and emotional problems and with time to give really adequate treatment. For the university, the service should aim to minimize the academic ill-effects of illness, and should advise tutors of individual students in difficulty; it should also conduct careful observation and research and be represented on the university's decision-making bodies so that it can play a part in making the climate of the university a healthy one. In this chapter I will examine how each of these aims may be achieved.

MEDICAL STAFFING

There is no formal postgraduate training for doctors wishing to work in university health services in Britain and those services which exist have recruited their staffs from elsewhere, initially from public health, general practice and general medicine, and latterly, increasingly from psychiatry also. There is a national shortage of psychiatrists and one cannot hope to have all psychiatric problems handled by specialists. In any case training in psychotherapy (which in the university context is the most relevant skill) is still rudimentary for many psychiatrists. Doctors from any background, if suitably selected for temperament and interest, and if given additional training, continuing case seminars and individual supervision, can soon learn which cases to treat themselves and which to refer, and can gradually extend the range of problems which they can handle themselves. The prime role of a psychiatrist in a university health service should be a teaching and supervisory one, his role in giving therapy being secondary to the running of training seminars, and the provision of consultation and case supervision.

If the basic staffing of the service consists of doctors with general practice or general medical background, these doctors will usually register students as patients under the National Health Service and be responsible for their day-to-day medical care. From the point of view of picking up the student in need of psychiatric help this system has many advantages when compared to those which demand formal referral for psychiatric care, and even more markedly when compared to those where psychiatric or counselling services operate independently of the medical services. A student's first approach may be tentative and both he and the doctor may need time before reaching a decision as to whether psychotherapy is indicated. Where the medical officers are all to some degree psychiatrically sophisticated, this tentative contact can be maintained until doctor and patient have made up their minds. Once a patient is taken on for formal psychotherapy, however, there may be a case for handing over general medical care to a colleague, as in some cases the patient's reactions to his therapist can interfere with some aspects of general medical care.

Many university health services are staffed largely by part-time doctors and this is inevitable in the newer, developing centres. There is, however, a desirable tendency towards whole-time staffing, and in my view doctors should give at least half of their time to their university work. Without this level of involvement in the work it is very difficult to understand the environment adequately or to become part of the university scene.

ANCILLARY STAFFING

Non-medical student counsellors and psychotherapists, working in a team with doctors and psychiatrists, can play an important part in the university setting, but adequately trained lay therapists are still comparatively rare in Britain. Clinical psychologists, who are less rare, do not in general, in this country, operate as therapists but they have an important role to play in the assessment of cases for therapy and in particular in the testing of the student in academic difficulty.

Nursing in the university context consists, in part, of 'casualty' care for minor ailments, but, especially if the sick-bay is used for psychiatric patients, some psychiatric skill is called for. With the right nurse and the right supervision the understanding support of the sick-bay sister can be an important part of the care of the more severely disturbed student. Finally, receptionists and secretaries play a large part both in maintaining the smooth running of the service and in projecting an impression of it to students and to faculty; these human skills should be emphasized in the selection of personnel.

ACCESSIBILITY AND CONFIDENTIALITY

In a service providing general care, the majority of students with psychiatric problems will find their way into psychiatric treatment on their own (that is to say they will be self-referred). As indicated above, their first approach may be a tentative one and the definite request for help or definite offer from the doctor may not be made until a number of contacts have taken place. The doctor, at this stage, must give full attention to physical symptoms but must also show that he is somebody with whom one could discuss emotional problems. Not every student who consults with an emotionally-based symptom will need treatment; half or more will have minor problems and will recover spontaneously.

Tutors represent another important source of referral. How many students consult as the result of their tutor's encouragement will depend upon how far the tutors understand and accept the role of the health service. The doctors must aim to extend this understanding as far as possible, so that not only are students with obvious emotional problems referred, but in addition, the floundering student or the student who fails to attend tutorials or hand in essays will be encouraged to consult, if only for assessment. In my own university, in addition to direct tutor referrals, any student who is experiencing serious academic difficulty (to an extent involving report to the Student Progress Committee) is sent a letter suggesting such a consultation, and nearly half of those so invited do attend. There is clearly no point in introducing any form of compulsion in this referral, but the practice is useful in establishing the role of the service in assessing individual problems. A major task of the service is to overcome, as far as possible, the suspicion and fear of psychiatry in students and faculty. The best agent for achieving this is the tutor, who, having referred a case, finds that the report he receives from the doctor is of real use to him and of help to the student. It is essential at all times to establish very clearly that the doctors will only discuss students who have given express permission. Most students in academic difficulty will give such permission but a few, quite often the more seriously disturbed, may withhold it.

Friends are a third source of referral. The student who notices an unusually prolonged depression or a change in behaviour in a friend, or the student made anxious by the demands or threats of another may try to persuade the disturbed person to consult. If he steadfastly refuses to attend, the friend may come to the doctor for advice on what to do. Unless there seems to be a real risk of suicide the doctor can usually do no more than invite the disturbed student to consult and very often even this cannot be done as the friends have come without telling the person involved. Where this is so it is usually best to suggest that they go directly to the potential patient and tell him of their concern and of the consultation with the doctor. There are occasions, of course, when it is the complaining friend rather than the one complained of who seems most in need of help.

Consultation with the friends of students who are already in treatment is more tricky for the doctor. He may listen to what they have to say, though preferably only when the patient knows of the consultation, but he is clearly bound not to discuss what he knows in confidence about his patient.

Confidentiality and Parents

I have emphasized above that neither friends nor tutors may be given information about students by the doctors, unless express permission is granted. In the case of parents the same caution is called for. Many parents assume that they have the right to be informed of any illness in their children and they are often resentful when they discover that this has not happened. Their disquiet is reinforced by the fact that some hospitals and doctors do insist upon informing relatives about patients under twenty-one. The legal position is in fact quite explicit; anyone aged sixteen or over has the right to medical confidentiality. In the context of university medicine there are frequently occasions when students explicitly insist that their parents should not be informed. One thinks particularly of cases of pregnancy and abortion, and of the psychiatrically disturbed student who has major emotional conflicts with his family. These students must know before they consult that their consultations are confidential, for if they do not know this they will feel unable to seek advice at all. It is very important that parents should understand this. Naturally in the majority of cases students will inform their parents of illness and in many cases in which they fear to do so the fear may be ill-founded. In such cases the doctor may discuss the basis of this fear and may suggest that it might be better to communicate, but he can go no further than that.

TUTOR / DOCTOR COMMUNICATION

Communication between doctors and tutors requires both organization and the continuing exercise of tact and skill. The machinery developed will depend upon the structure of the university. In my own, we have evolved a two-way system of liaison in each school of study – schools being the basic teaching unit at Sussex. In other universities the department or the college might be a more appropriate unit. Each school appoints one faculty member to be liaison officer with the health service and all communications about individual students, whether from doctor to tutor or from tutor to doctor are channelled through him. The school liaison officers are also members of the Health Service Advisory Committee. In addition, each doctor takes on a special responsibility for certain specific schools, so that any general queries arising in these schools about health service practice can be channelled through him and he will be available for informal discussions with tutors in that school.

Contacts over individual cases are made and maintained through this machinery, but the use made of the contact is primarily to ensure that the tutor in day-to-day teaching contact with the student who has problems can discuss these problems with the doctor looking after him. These discussions may serve to do no more than alert the tutor to vulnerability in the student or cover the student who has got behind through illness. But in other cases it may be that the psychopathology of the student has got deeply involved in the teaching situation, as in the cases described in Chapter 8. In this case it may be important to help tutors to avoid exacerbation of, or collusion with, neurotic forms of interaction with the student.

Good tutor/doctor communication (and one could add good tutor/tutor and doctor/doctor communication) is most essential when one encounters the manipulative patient. The student who assures his doctor that the tutor is an incompetent ass with no understanding of people ('unlike you Dr A . . . .') or the student who asks his tutor to rescue him from the psychoanalytic clutches of the health centre ('what I really need is your common sense and sympathy Mr X . . .') is inviting the other to join in the game which analysts call splitting. Splitting implies a sharp polarization of attitudes to people or events in the patient's life. Commonly it involves using people to play the fantasy roles of good versus bad parent or kind, affectionate versus dangerous sexual partner. At times the highly developed player (that is, the deeply disturbed individual) goes beyond splitting to fragmentation by involving numerous others, as in the following case.

Case History

A male arts student had received psychiatric treatment before coming to university. Within ten days of his arrival he had consulted the university health service and within three weeks was in psychotherapy, delighted that he had at last found 'somebody who could really understand him'. His problems were based upon early childhood deprivation, associated with the loss of his father at the age of four. His difficulties were briefly assuaged but later exacerbated by a deeply involved affair with a married student during his second term. Through this period treatment remained gratefully accepted, but in his third term he abandoned the married student and turned against his therapist, the sessions becoming angry and silent.

He now switched for his main support to an ex-schoolteacher, who had long been 'in reserve' but who was now promoted to a key position. He was willing to give him much time, even travelling down to see him when summoned, but he saw him as somebody unable to cope with his most depressed and angry parts 'because he was so sensitive'. Additional supports were therefore extracted from his personal tutor. His evening visits to his office, always made as he was on the point of leaving, were so persistent that he resorted to taking him home 'to help bath the children'. During his first long vacation his home doctor was persuaded to refer him to another psychiatrist near the university and he somewhat triumphantly abandoned his therapist on returning at the start of his second year. However, three months later there was an acute crisis in which he returned to his health service therapist asking for support. At this time, over the course of three days, he also summoned the teacher and drew in no less than three tutors who contacted the health service on his behalf.

Coping with this type of behaviour is extremely difficult. In this case the man's genuine deprivation and distress evoked from each person involved a supportive or affirmative response of some sort, but he was not able to accept from anyone more than a small part of a relationship and the moment a check or a disappointment was experienced, his affection and need were replaced by anger, and comfort was extracted from someone else. The moral of this story is simple in principle but complex in practice; beware the individual who makes one into someone special and who contrasts one's virtues and strengths with another's vices and weaknesses. Such a person is inviting one to confirm their neurosis and to perpetuate their inability to achieve a whole relationship.

In general, people of this sort try to ensure that the different actors in their drama remain unknown to each other. One aim of tutor/doctor co-operation is precisely to minimize this process and ultimately this must be done by direct communication between the individuals involved. This can only occur in the university if some insights about this and other psychodynamic mechanisms are successfully disseminated among faculty.

PSYCHIATRY FOR TUTORS?

There is, understandably, in the minds of many people a resistance to psychiatric and especially psychodynamic concepts, and particularly in the intellectually rigorous academic atmosphere of a university the tender and apparently unscientific shoots of psychoanalysis are exposed to a cold wind, so cold indeed that there is often no growth even within the health service. Resistance here will seldom be overcome by ideological confrontation or by patient logical expositions of theory (which is not to say there is no place within the discipline for more rigorous formulations of the theories). The most persuasive argument, as I have suggested above, is the success of the service in helping students. This argument can, however, be backed up by more formal methods, in particular by arranging seminars or conferences at which tutors and doctors can jointly discuss particular problems. The tutors who are attracted by such seminars will often be those already interested and favourably disposed, and will include those who have already shared problem students with the doctors. The aim of the meetings will be to relate the experience of the doctor treating and the tutor teaching to what is going on 'inside' the student, and to help the tutor see the ways in which the student's attitudes to them or to the teaching situation can be derived from unconscious, irrational processes. These discussions also serve to clarify for tutors the type of problem which can appropriately be referred for medical treatment, and indeed they are often followed by a higher tutor referral rate. Sometimes a tutor may discover things in himself that exacerbate certain students' problems; perhaps over-involvement or perhaps remoteness, or some more complex aspect. Generally, though, such an awareness of his own contribution to the student's difficulty will only emerge in the course of continuing seminar discussions.

It needs to be emphasized that the aim of this work with tutors is not to make them into therapists, but to help them to *be* tutors, freed as far as possible from the interference and distraction of neurotic interaction with the student.

THE HEALTH SERVICE IN THE UNIVERSITY STRUCTURE

In the last section I have discussed communication between doctors and tutors. There are two other areas in which the relationship of health service to university needs further definition; the place of research and the representation of the service on university committees.

Research is not an essential function of every service, except in the modest sense that every university will want to be informed, to some extent, of its state of health through basic morbidity statistics. There are, however, many opportunities for more subtle studies of individuals in the university community and wider opportunities for research into the problems of the adolescent and into the border country between psychiatry and education. These opportunities have not, until now, been much exploited in Britain but the picture is beginning to change. In my view the doctor working in an academic setting should be encouraged to function academically by carrying out research. The university vacations, during which the clinical load upon the doctors is greatly reduced, offer a practical opportunity for such research which is denied to many doctors working in other contexts.

As regards representation on university committees the voice of the health service should, in my view, be heard upon the university Senate and on other bodies engaged in the consideration of general social problems and policy, and of specific students in difficulty. Effective discussions about the basic issues of student health and about teaching problems will take place at less elevated levels, but it is on these committees that the role of the health service within the university community will be defined.

COSTS AND BENEFITS

In the majority of British student health services giving general practice care under the National Health Service, the staff are salaried and pay their capitation and other health service moneys back to the university. In such a service, the cost per student per year, excluding buildings, runs between £3 and £7 of which sum about £3 can be recouped from the National Health Service. Variations in cost are largely accounted for by the scope of the service provided and in particular by the extent of psychiatric treatment available. If local facilities for psychiatry are good, as may be the case if there is a medical school in the university, or if psychotherapy is not carried out by the service, the cost will be lower.

The total cost of keeping a student at university in any one year is estimated to run at £700 to £1,000 so even at the upper limit the health service share of expenditure does not exceed one per cent. Is this expenditure justified?

The real costing of the service is impossible to calculate accurately, but in strict economic terms there are certain definite benefits. In so far as psychiatric intervention can reduce academic under-achievement and can diminish the waste of tutors' time due to neurotic work difficulties in students, then some of the medical time paid for can be off-set against tutorial time saved. Similarly the backing-up of the tutor's 'moral' or personal tutor function by the health service is a safeguard against the tutor becoming involved in intensive and unrewarding attempts to cope with a severely disturbed student. If a student can be prevented from withdrawing by psychiatric intervention, or if a student can be advised to withdraw over a period of incapacity, the waste of university resources will be diminished. Reference to the figure given above for the annual cost of a student place will show how even a small reduction in wastage rates could cover the costs of a health service, if one assumes (which is perhaps not entirely justified) that the expenditure on a student withdrawing after a year can be largely written off.

This economic justification for the provision of an adequate university health service cannot be considered proven because of the lack of knowledge about all the other factors influencing student wastage or under-achievement and because of the absence of controlled observations of the effects of psychiatric intervention. There are, however, other claims which in my view justify the provision of these services and indeed which point to the need for their expansion. The values of modern society and of the modern educational system are easily felt to be more economic than human. The economic arguments given above for the provision of a health service could equally easily have been arguments for improving the maintenance service of a factory producing manufactured goods. The existence of a university health service concerned essentially with individual welfare is one of the ways in which the conveyor-belt atmosphere of the modern educational system can be diminished. In this context, it is worth recalling what was said earlier, that over half the psychiatric work carried out in a university health service is concerned with students who are functioning satisfactorily academically but unsatisfactorily as people.

Apart from providing a service which shows concern for individual needs, doctors working in a university setting can influence the attitudes of the community by spreading an awareness and understanding of the unconscious factors in human behaviour. In so doing, they can play a part in ensuring that, however complex our society and however powerful the development of rational activities, the individual's needs, his uniqueness and his value as an individual are not forgotten. If the university recognizes the variability, the vulnerability, and the irrationality of its members, if it shows understanding for the difficult and concern for the casualty, may one not hope that its graduates will go into the world more able likewise to show recognition, understanding and concern for their fellows in other communities and institutions? As Henry Maudsley wrote in 1883, '. . . the intellect is aristocratic and the heart democratic, knowledge puffing up but love uniting and building up, and the true social problem is to democratise the intellect through the heart.'

References

1. BAKER, R. W., 'Incidence of Psychological Disturbances in College Students', *Journal of the American College Health Association*, vol. 13, 1963, p. 532.
2. BANNISTER, D., 'The Rationale and Clinical Relevance of Repertory Grid Technique', *British Journal of Psychiatry*, vol. 111, 1965, p. 977.
3. BANNISTER, D. and MAIR, J. M. M., *The Evaluation of Personal Constructs*, Academic Press, 1968.
4. BARRACLOUGH, B. M. and KREITMAN, N. B., 'Mental Hospital Admissions in England and Wales 1950–1960', *Monthly Bulletin of the Health and Public Health Laboratory Service*, vol. 26, 1967, p. 63.
5. BURTON, ROBERT, *The Anatomy of Melancholy*, 1621.
6. CARPENTER, R. G., 'Statistical Analysis of Suicide and Morbidity Rates of Students', *British Journal of Preventive and Social Medicine*, vol. 13, 1959, p. 163.
7. CLARK, B. R. and TROW, M. in *College Peer Groups*, eds. Newcombe, T. M. and Wilson, E. K., Aldine Publishing Co., Chicago, 1966.
8. CURTIS, J. R. and CURTIS, T. E., 'A Study of Drop Outs at the University of North Carolina', *Journal of the American College Health Association*, vol. 14, 1966, p. 140.
9. DANIEL, K. B., 'A Study of College Drop Outs with Respect to Academic and Personality Variables', *Journal of Educational Research*, vol. 60 (5), 1967, p. 230.
10. DAVIDSON, M. A. and HUTT, C., 'A Study of 500 Oxford Student Psychiatric Patients', *British Journal of Social and Clinical Psychology*, vol. 3, 1964, p. 175.
11. DAVIDSON, M. A., PARNELL, R. W. and SPENCER, S. J. G., 'The Detection of Psychological Vulnerability in Students', *Journal of Mental Science*, vol. 101, 1955, p. 810.
12. DAVY, B. W., 'The Sources and Prevention of Mental Ill Health in

University Students', *Proceedings of the Royal Society of Medicine*, vol. 53, 1960, p. 764.

13. DOUGLAS, J. W. B. and MULLIGAN, D. G., 'Emotional Adjustment and Educational Achievement', *Proceedings of the Royal Society of Medicine*, vol. 54, 1961, p. 885.

14. DREWS, E. M. and TEAHAR, J. E., 'Parental Attitudes and Academic Achievement', *Journal of Clinical Psychology*, vol. 13, 1957, p. 328.

15. ERIKSON, E., *Childhood and Society*, Norton, New York, 1950.

16. EYSENCK, H. J. and EYSENCK, B. G., *Manual of the Eysenck Personality Inventory*, University of London Press, 1964.

17. FARNSWORTH, D. L., *Psychiatry, Education and the Young Adult*, Thomas, Springfield, U.S.A., 1966.

18. FRYER, D., 'A Map of the Underground', *Encounter*, vol. 24 (4), 1967, p. 6.

19. FURNEAUX, W. D., 'The Too Few Chosen and the Many That Could Be Called', *Sociological Review Monograph No. 7*, ed. Halmos, Keele University, 1963.

20. FURNEAUX, W. D., *Manual of the Nufferno Speed Tests*, University of London Press, 1965.

21. HEILBRUN, A. B., 'Parental Identification and College Adjustment', *Psychological Reports*, vol. 10, 1962, p. 853.

22. HEILBRUN, A. B., 'Sex Role Identity and Achievement Motivation', *Psychological Reports*, vol. 12, 1963, p. 483.

23. HILL, A. H., 'A Longitudinal Study of Attrition Among High Aptitude College Students', *Journal of Educational Research*, vol. 60 (4), 1966, p. 166.

24. HIMMELWEIT, H., 'Student Selection', *Sociological Review Monograph No. 7*, ed. Halmos, Keele University, 1963.

25. HUDSON, L., 'Academic Sheep and Research Goats', *New Society*, 22 October 1964.

26. HUDSON, L., *Contrary Imaginations*, Methuen, London, 1966.

27. HUDSON, L., *Selection and the Problem of Conformity* in *Genetic and Environmental Factors in Human Ability*, eds. Meade and Parkes, Oliver and Boyd, Edinburgh, 1966.

28. KELLY, G. A., *The Psychology of Personal Constructs* (2 vols.), Norton, New York, 1955.

29. KELVIN, R. P., LUCAS, C. J. and OJHA, A. B., 'Personality, Mental Health and Academic Performance', *British Journal of Social and Clinical Psychology*, vol. 4, 1965, p. 42.

30. KESSEL, N. and SHEPHERD, M., 'Neurosis in Hospital and General Practice', *Journal of Mental Science*, vol. 108, 1962, p. 159.

31. KIDD, C. B., 'Psychiatric Morbidity Among Students', *British Journal of Preventive and Social Medicine*, vol. 19, 1965, p. 143.

32. KIDD, C. B. and CALDBECK-MEENAN, J., 'A Comparative Study of Psychiatric Morbidity Among Students of Two Different Universities', *British Journal of Psychiatry*, vol. 112, 1966, p. 57.

33. LAING, R. D., *The Divided Self*, Tavistock Publications, 1959.

34. LAING, R. D., *The Self and Others*, Tavistock Publications, 1961.

35. LAING, R. D., *The Politics of Experience and the Bird of Paradise*, Penguin Books, 1967.

36. LAING, R. D. and ESTERSON, A., 'Sanity, Madness and the Family', *Families of Schizophrenics* (vol. 1), Tavistock Publications, 1964.

37. LIDZ, T., 'Schizophrenia and the Family', *Psychiatry*, vol. 21, 1958, p. 21.

38. LUCAS, C. J., KELVIN, R. P. and OJHA, A. B., 'Mental Health and Student Wastage', *British Journal of Psychiatry*, vol. 112, 1966, p. 277.

39. MALLESON, N., *A Handbook on British Student Health Services*, Pitman Medical Publishing Co., 1964.

40. MALLESON, N., 'Panic and Phobia', *Lancet*, vol. 1, 1959, p. 225.

41. MAUDSLEY, HENRY, *Body and Will*, Kegan Paul, French and Co., London, 1883.

42. MISHLER, E. G. and WAXLER, N. E., 'Family Interaction Processes and Schizophrenia – A Review of Current Theories', *International Journal of Psychiatry*, vol. 2, 1961, p. 375.

43. PERVIN, L. A., 'Identification, Identity and the College Drop Out', *Journal of the American College Health Association*, vol. 14, 1966, p. 158.

44. PIRANDELLO, L., *Right You Are! (If You Think So)*, Penguin Books, 1962.

45. POWELL, D. H., 'The Return of the Drop Out', *Journal of the American College Health Association*, vol. 13, 1965, p. 475.

46. ROWNTREE, G., 'New Facts on Teenage Marriage', *New Society*, 4 October 1962.

47. Royal College of Physicians of London, *Report* of the Social and Preventive Medicine Committee Subcommittee on the Student Health Service, 1966.

48. RYLE, A., *Neurosis in the Ordinary Family*, Tavistock Publications, London, 1967

49. RYLE, A., 'Clinical Observations on the Relationship of Academic Difficulty to Psychiatric Illness', *British Journal of Psychiatry*, vol. 114, 1968, p. 755.

50. RYLE, A. and LUNGHI, M., 'A Psychometric Study of Academic

Difficulty and Psychiatric Illness in Students', *British Journal of Psychiatry*, vol. 114, 1968, p. 57.

51. SCHOFIELD, M., *The Sexual Behaviour of Young People*, Longmans, 1965.

52. SLATER, P., 'The Use of the Repertory Grid Technique on the Individual Case', *British Journal of Psychiatry*, vol. 111, p. 965.

53. SNYDER, B. R., 'How Does the Educator Under Stress Align his Personal and Professional Priorities?', *Current Issues on Higher Education*, vol. 40, 1965.

54. SNYDER, B. R., 'Creative Students in Science and Engineering', Address to *Conference on Creativity and Higher Education at Center for Study of Higher Education, University of California*, Berkeley, 1966.

55. SPIEGEL, J. P. and BELL, N. W., 'The Family of the Psychiatric Patient', *The American Handbook of Psychiatry*, ed. Arieti, New York Basie Books, 1959.

56. STENGEL, E., *Suicide and Attempted Suicide*, Penguin Books, 1964.

57. STILL, R. T., *The Mental Health of Students*, University of Leeds Student Health Service, 1966.

58. SUMMERSKILL, J., 'Drop Outs from College', in *The American College*, Wiley & Sons, New York, 1962.

59. TRUAX, C. B. and WARGO, D. G., 'Psychotherapeutic Encounters that Change Behaviour: For Better or For Worse', *American Journal of Psychotherapy*, vol. 20, 1966, p. 499.

60. VERNON, P., 'The Pool of Ability', *Sociological Review Monograph No. 7*, ed. Halmos, Keele University, 1963.

61. WATTS, A. W., *The Joyous Cosmology*, Vintage Books (Random), New York, 1962.

Index

Index

More about Penguins and Pelicans

Penguinews, which appears every month, contains details of all the new books issued by Penguins as they are published. From time to time it is supplemented by *Penguins in Print*, which is a complete list of all available books published by Penguins. (There are well over three thousand of these.)

A specimen copy of *Penguinews* will be sent to you free on request, and you can become a subscriber for the price of the postage. For a year's issues (including the complete lists) please send 30p if you live in the United Kingdom, or 60p if you live elsewhere. Just write to Dept EP, Penguin Books Ltd, Harmondsworth, Middlesex, enclosing a cheque or postal order, and your name will be added to the mailing list.

Note: *Penguinews* and *Penguins in Print* are not available in the U.S.A. or Canada

The Psychotic

Understanding Madness

Andrew Crowcroft

'Am I mad?'

Consciously or unconsciously, this agonizing question has been asked by millions of those who, for any reason, have felt themselves to be set apart from others in their childhood. Madness provides one of the commonest unfounded fears of neurotics.

A consultant psychiatrist explains in this study, as exactly as the condition permits, what madness is. Drawing a clear line between psychosis and neurosis, he takes us into the world of madness by two paths; first through a survey of what specialists now know about psychotic breakdown, and secondly through a brilliant comparison between broken patterns of thought and feeling in childhood and the shattered world of the psychotic. The author interprets much experience and behaviour on the lines of Melanie Klein's theory of early emotional development and admits, through her, a debt to Freud. But Freud specialized in the psycho-neuroses.

And Dr Crowcroft's book, with its clear outline of social and physical treatments available today, is concerned with psychosis – true madness – in a way which has not previously been attempted in a popular edition.

The Unattached

Mary Morse

Resentment, apathy, mistrust – the dead-end job, the Beat sound, and a rejection of the values of adult society. These are the kind of words with which journalists have tried to catch and understand the unattached – the teenagers who don't belong to anyone or anything. What kind of people are they? What are their attitudes, needs, aims, or resentments? How can they be approached or understood?

In 1960 the National Association of Youth Clubs set up a pioneer experiment to discover the answers to these questions and possible solutions to the problem of the unattached. Three young social workers were sent, each to a different town, under concealed identities, to find and to scrape an acquaintance with those particular teenagers. Over three years, the three, one of whom was a young woman, eventually became the trusted friends and confidants of the bored, the apathetic, the rebellious, and the defiant. This account of the workers' experiences offers an utterly authentic insight into the world of the unattached. But the book is more than this: it is also a fascinating description of difficulties, loneliness, fears, and setbacks of three social workers, working out on a limb in isolation and under assumed identities. It is a fascinating account of a remarkable experiment.